Visitors to the House of Memory

Museums and Collections

Editors

Mary Bouquet, University College Utrecht, and
Howard Morphy, The Australian National University, Canberra

As houses of memory and sources of information about the world, museums function as a dynamic interface between past, present and future. Museum collections are increasingly being recognized as material archives of human creativity and as invaluable resources for interdisciplinary research. Museums provide powerful forums for the expression of ideas and are central to the production of public culture: they may inspire the imagination, generate heated emotions and express conflicting values in their material form and histories. This series explores the potential of museum collections to transform our knowledge of the world, and for exhibitions to influence the way in which we view and inhabit that world. It offers essential reading for those involved in all aspects of the museum sphere: curators, researchers, collectors, students and the visiting public.

Visitors to the House of Memory

Identity and Political Education at the Jewish Museum Berlin

Victoria Bishop Kendzia

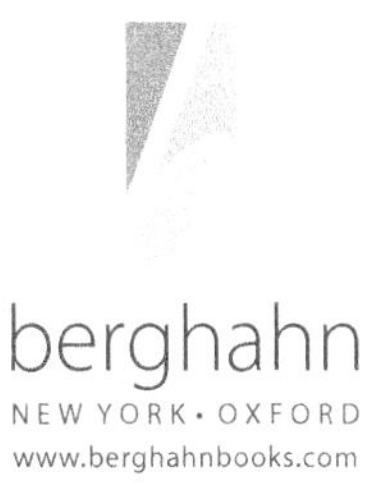

berghahn
NEW YORK • OXFORD
www.berghahnbooks.com

Library of Congress Cataloging-in-Publication Data

Names: Bishop Kendzia, Victoria, author.
Title: Visitors to the house of memory : identity and political education at the
  Jewish Museum Berlin / Victoria Bishop Kendzia.
Description: 1st edition. | New York : Berghahn Books, [2018] | Series:
  Museums and collections ; Volume 9 | Includes bibliographical references
  and index.
Identifiers: LCCN 2017051485 (print) | LCCN 2017052700 (ebook) | ISBN
  9781785336409 (eBook) | ISBN 9781785336393 (hardback : alk. paper)
Subjects: LCSH: Judisches Museum Berlin (1999–). | Holocaust, Jewish
  (1939–1945)—Museums—Europe. | Jewish museums—Germany—Berlin. |
  Holocaust memorials—Germany—Berlin.
Classification: LCC D804.175.B4 (ebook) | LCC D804.175.B4 B57 2018
  (print) | DDC 940.53/1807443155—dc23
LC record available at https://lccn.loc.gov/2017051485

British Library Cataloguing in Publication Data

A catalogue record for this book is available from the British Library

ISBN 978-1-78533-639-3 hardback
ISBN 978-1-78920-844-3 paperback
ISBN 978-1-78533-640-9 ebook

In loving memory of Konstantin Kendzia and Michael E. Bishop

CONTENTS

Illustrations

Acknowledgments

The list of those who have helped and supported me along this path, which now culminates in this manuscript, is long. I would like, however, to single out a few institutions and individuals, without which this journey would not have been possible. Thank you to the staff in visitor services and education at the Jewish Museum Berlin for their openness, input, and invaluable support, not to mention to the many guides and other staff members who answered my questions and concerns throughout the research process. Thank you too to the many teachers, who took time out of their school schedules to accommodate the visits and interviews, and who also participated actively in the process. The biggest thank-you, however, is owed to the pupils themselves who undertook this project with me and have been so important in helping me to explore the issues and my own place within them.

Naturally, the support of the Institute for European Ethnology at Humboldt University, Berlin, where I have been warmly welcomed, has been crucial. The encouraging input and constructive criticism offered by colleagues there has been of the highest quality and very much appreciated. Thank you to Wolfgang Kaschuba, Joachim Kallinich; Sharon Macdonald and Robin Ostow for their time and much valued advice throughout these years. Thank you too to Jackie Feldman for his very valuable and constructive input and to Irit Dekel for her advice and empathy over the years. Many friends and colleagues have also opened up new avenues of inquiry to me, which have proven decisive in my own analyses. Finally, none of this would have been possible without my husband's loving patience, and intellectual contributions, and my children's willingness to share their mother with this project.

Preface

The choice of topic comes out of my background in history and museum studies, and my belief that museums, as purveyors of history and culture, can reflect and influence their environments. The choice of the Jewish Museum Berlin (JMB), though, is a personal one. Growing up in Canada in the 1980s, the topic of World War II and the Holocaust was a small part of my formal education and a larger part of the general popular culture. In my home, the remembrance was more significant. My mother would often reminisce about the painful events of her childhood in London during the war. This included first growing up on a farm and believing she was the daughter of the loving Christian couple who cared for her. She would, at times, describe to my brothers and myself the very traumatic event of being collected by two sophisticated-sounding adults from London and being told that she was not who she thought she was: she was their child and she was Jewish, with all the implications that this new identity had for her. My parents did not raise us in any religious tradition, although my brothers and I attended a French Catholic school (my father was nominally Catholic). Consequently, I neither perceived myself nor was seen by others as Jewish. Nevertheless, I always had some knowledge of these roots and was aware of how the tragedy of the last century touched my mother's side of the family. Indeed, when the topic of the Holocaust came up in personal conversations, as it did occasionally, or in television and media events, as it did much more often, there was no question of which "side" I was on. Occasionally, as a teenager, I lamented not being free to identify solely with the victors (in this case the British military and political forces) to which my antecedents on both sides also had clear connections.

Having moved to Germany in 2001, to be with my German (non-Jewish) husband, and having two daughters, has more recently sparked my interest specifically in how Jewish history is negotiated here, while also re-awakening issues of flexible, shifting identity for myself and my approach to child rearing. Into what kind of culture of memory am I raising my children? What are the implications of their backgrounds in how this difficult legacy might be approached? I found it remarkable that a "Jewish" museum could find a home here in Berlin and be so successfully received. I was initially suspicious of the German government's plan to build such a museum, wondering if it might merely constitute a weak attempt at *Wiedergutmachen* (making things good again): a "German" space, with idealized, imaginary Jews. I hesitated some time before actually visiting the museum. The museum itself opened in 2001 (shortly after my relocation to Berlin). The planning and construction of the museum was a long and troubled affair stretching over decades. It entailed a great deal of acrimonious public debate in the German and international media. Indeed, while I was completing my master of museum studies degree in Toronto in 1999, there was discussion there about the upcoming JMB and Daniel Libeskind's daring design. It was, in fact, my father who finally convinced me to go with him during one of his visits to Berlin. I was surprised at the design of the museum and have come to see that the doubts that I harbored are built into the very architecture and have been shared by others involved in the process. I also felt that its dual nature as memorial and museum had a particular poignancy and pedagogical potential. The choice of which groups to focus on for the study—Berlin-based senior high school students—with interest in history—offers an opportunity to explore how this history might be carried over to the next generation in Germany by those most actively interested in it. It is precisely this, which is so crucial for me to explore, as I hope to pass on to my daughters a balanced understanding of what it can mean to contemplate this past.

Introduction

I think it fitting to outline two key contextual issues, dilemmas in fact, regarding the manner in which the museum positions itself that I encountered very early on in the process, as these should help to frame the concerns that arose. First, in preparation for conducting my own research, I read the extensive work on Holocaust memorials by James Young. In his chapter outlining the history of this museum, Young (2000) cited the conceptual brief authored by Rolf Bothe (the then director of the Berlin Museum) and Vera Bendt (the then director of the Jewish department of the Berlin Museum) for the design competition, which Daniel Libeskind later won. "Nothing in Berlin's history ever changed the city more than the persecution, expulsion, and murder of its own Jewish citizens. This change worked inwardly, affecting the very heart of the city" (Young 2000: 161). These lines struck me at the time and have remained with me ever since. Initially, I read this statement matter-of-factly and was astonished. I just did not see this interpretation being shared at all around me, either in conversations or in historical texts. (Surely, I thought, the destruction of Berlin during World War II, or its being forcibly split asunder for decades afterward, would be deemed as, if not more, significant than the loss of its Jews?)

I imagined I would be hard pressed to find more than a handful of Berliners that would honestly sign the statement written by Rolf Bothe and Vera Bendt, let alone a consensus. Coming to see this text as part of a performative public relations campaign, however, allowed me to better cope with, if not resolve, the dilemma. Rather than a statement reflecting a consensus, it is much more a message that the authors wanted to send about Germany through the potential design of this museum. This statement was about projecting an image of Germany. Perhaps the authors personally believed it too, as others might.[1] But whether or not there was a consensus among actual "Germans" seems beside the point. It, nevertheless, remains problematic that the authors claimed the legitimacy to speak on Germany's behalf, as if it were one national monolith. In dealing with such material then, it is even more crucial not to conflate public discourse on memory with actually shared memory (cf. Young 1993: xi).

Next, as my own impression of this museum was very much connected to memory of the Holocaust, the assertion by Ken Gorbey, the then project manager of the exhibition that the Jewish Museum Berlin (JMB) was "not a Holocaust memorial" (Gorbey 2002: 9) also seemed of place. This is made explicit in the museum's mission statement:

> The museum is not a Holocaust memorial. Rather we present a view of German Jewish history that is balanced between, on the one hand, celebration of the ordinary and extraordinary lives of all generations and, on the other, the recognition and explication of the darker side of that history. (Gorbey 2002: 9)

To contextualize this statement, it is helpful to review some aspects in the long and tortured history of this museum's coming into being. Originally proposed as an extension to the existing Berlin Museum, with Heinz Galinski (1912–92), then president of West Berlin's Jewish community, as its champion, the process of making the JMB went through many arduous phases, too involved to report in full here. A few points, however, are worth emphasizing. From its onset, this extension was not conceived as a Holocaust museum. In fact, this topic was hardly reflected at all in original concepts (cf. Ostow 2007: 310; Pieper 2006: 213, 224, 230). It was with the choice of the design proposal by Daniel Libeskind that this changed dramatically (cf. Ostow 2007: 310–11; Pieper 2006: 232). Katrin Pieper points out that:

> With their decision, the jury laid the groundwork for the public assessment of the Libeskind-Bau as a "space memorializing" both the extermination and Jewish life in Berlin, as both a "carrier of historical meaning" and a "Holocaust memorial." (2006: 236)[2]

Indeed this structure was largely read as a Holocaust memorial (cf. Kessler 2001: 97; Ostow 2007: 309). Julius Schoeps, a prominent German-Jewish historian and political scientist, even suggested keeping it as a Holocaust memorial and housing the museum elsewhere (Ostow 2007: 310; Pieper 2006: 243). There followed an acrimonious conflict, which came to a head over plans by the body then in charge of the Berlin Museum, the *Stiftung Stadtmuseum Berlin* (City Museum Foundation Berlin, a local governmental body staffed by non-Jewish Germans), to relegate the Jewish section to the basement. This horrified members of the Jewish community who then felt compelled to become more actively involved in the process fearing that relegation to the basement—the dark, somber sections of the building— leaving the brighter upper floors to house Berlin German history, might even cause an increase in anti-Semitism (Pieper 2006: 249*ff.*). Clearly then tensions arose early in the process in connection to a number of factors, which include the very makeup of the building.

The conflicts resulted in an impasse, as the opposing memories of this history (namely the perceptions of the Jewish community versus the German *Stiftung*'s position) could not be reconciled. The *Stiftung Stadtmuseum Berlin* under Rainer Güntzer stood on one side, and the, now actively and publicly involved, Berlin Jewish community, on the other. Acrimony was widely reported in the press: Rainer Güntzer characterized the present-day Jewish opponents to the *Stiftung*'s plans for the museum as unpatriotic and not good Germans. While they fired back accusing him of complete and utter insensitivity to their experience and memory, not to mention of only being interested in dead Jews, while ignoring the needs of the living. The unceremonious firing of the Israeli director of the Jewish Department of the Berlin Museum, Amnon Barzel, by the *Stiftung Stadtmuseum* only further exacerbated the conflict.[3] The deadlock lasted until a political solution could be found from the outside: enter W. Michael Blumenthal, a one-time member of the Berlin Jewish Community, who had fled to Shanghai after the November 1938 Pogrom. He became successful in America in business and politics, serving as secretary of the treasury under President Carter. It was in part his managerial and negotiating skills, coupled with his irreproachable credentials that allowed the process to move forward. He was able to secure the museum exclusively for the Jewish topic, effectively sidelining the *Stiftung Stadtmuseum,* and turning this museum into a national German museum about Jews with federal funding (cf. Ostow 2007: 311; Pieper 2006: 283).

Early on in the exhibition planning, there was a strong optimistic note struck: Ken Gorbey stated, "We want happy visitors!" (Broder 2001: 266) and "We don't want to ignore the concept of perpetration, but to visit a guilt trip upon the German people is not the objective of this museum" (Klein 2001: 3). While W. Michael Blumenthal admitted the difficulty of this optimistic position: "If they would have called me before they built this building, I would have likely tried to negotiate with Daniel Libeskind to build it a bit differently" (Minutes of the Committee of Cultural Affairs, 9th Meeting, 19 June 2000, Parliament of Berlin, 14th legislative period, in Senate Department, VAI, Jewish Museum Concept, p. 15; Pieper 2006: 298 n. 825).[4]

Candid admissions of the disconnect between the architecture and the museum's preferred label: "not a Holocaust museum" were also offered to me in an interview with a member of the education department of the JMB. She conceded that in this building, it was impossible to not be a Holocaust museum, but that in their exhibitions and tours they tried to alternate the emphases and focus on other topics too (Interview 24 February 2011).

The institution calls itself the JMB. Its director W. Michael Blumenthal refers to it clearly as a "German history museum" (Blumenthal 2001: 1). Authentic artifacts are presented throughout the permanent exhibition and displayed in the underground axes along the walls. However, the *Libeskind-Bau,* with its evocative design, is in many ways a Holocaust memorial. The architect's idea was, as he put it: "very simple: to build the museum around a void that runs through it" (Libeskind 1991: 63). This void is meant to represent "a space empty of Jews," echoing an inner space empty of the love and values that might have saved them (Young 2000: 165). (Here one can see how this concept corresponds to the brief written by Bothe and Bendt.) I would argue then that the JMB should be understood—and is very often experienced—as a memorial museum. Paul Williams list the JMB as one site in his book appropriately entitled *Memorial Museums* (Williams 2007: 20). He recognizes too that such sites are "dedicated to commemorating mass suffering of some kind" (Williams 2007: 8). Thus, a moral and emotional tone is part of their makeup (Bishop Kendzia 2012: 81).

Such tensions and contradictions surrounding the museum's role accompanied the fieldwork throughout. My work is both ethnographic and auto-ethnographic, deliberately so. My aim is not only to share the insights gained, but also to introduce the readers to the museum and the visitors, as I experienced them over time. Auto-ethnography is crucial to mine the personal experiences throughout the process to render this text "meaningful, accessible, and evocative" (Ellis et al. 2011).[5] I have, therefore maintained some, at times, chronological narrative elements to accomplish this to enable the reader to view, and possibly identify with, my positioning throughout.

The book is organized as follows: Chapter 1 outlines the research question and the multifaceted methodology as they developed over time. With this, I hope to achieve a transparency and reflexivity that should help the reader to judge my findings appropriately. Chapter 2 outlines the key conceptual frameworks that inform the work. It discusses prevailing understandings of memory and political education as they pertain to this research, questioning the value of the idea of a shared memory in favor of performative models like remembrance (Jay Winter) and "past presencing" (Sharon Macdonald) as more useful tools. Indeed the visitors are performing with and for each other, the museum staff, and myself. This perspective is crucial to adequately analyze the situations that arose in their variety and complexity. This framework goes on to link remembrance to political education, more generally, and then focus on the situation in Germany and the JMB specifically, asking how and for whom political education is envisioned. This leads to an appreciation of the culture of memory in Germany as a product of a dominant discourse, in which certain young visitors operate masterfully, while others do not. Some visitors are clearly insiders and know the rules. Chapter 3 then accompanies these insiders in the museum and in the classroom. They experienced the museum largely as a Holocaust memorial space. Here expressions of guilt and dismay loom large, but so do pride, and very carefully considered utterances, implicit coercive expectations, and Holocaust fatigue. Chapter 4 introduces those visitors who perceived the museum far more as a tourist site, without expressing anything like guilt or the like. The conflicts and confusion this entailed in situ are telling: they expose assumptions of how Germans are supposed to remember, and recall that this country has a legacy of a divided nation with clear consequences in the present. In Chapter 5, we meet a school group from *Neukölln*—a part of Berlin with a majority population of Turkish background. The group was willing and eager to participate in this study. I had been told that many Muslim students, for example, have refused to visit the JMB since they equate it with "pro-Israel propaganda," and others have certainly experienced this (cf. Feldman and Peleikis 2014: 50). It did not present a problem in my case, however. We explore how their day out at the museum and the conflicts it produced point to a troubling fixed understanding of who belongs inside the culture of memory and who does not. This raises difficult questions regarding the possibilities of integration—that is finding a sense of belonging that allows for difference (as opposed to assimilation, which calls for the erasure of difference). Finally, the conclusion ties the important threads of the fieldwork together, interrogating the constellations of coercion, political correctness, dominance, and marginalization. It then aims to open up questions about the future of remembrance and belonging in the museum and beyond.

Notes

1. Also worth thinking about is the implied audience of this brief. Might it not also be the case that as often with artistic endeavor, and I would include museum exhibitions in this: "the perceived public audience is none other than [the creators] themselves" (Young 1993: 9).
2. All translations from German are, unless otherwise stated, my own. I apologize in advance for any errors as they are fully my own.
   Die Jury legte mit ihrem Urteil die Grundlage für die öffentliche Bewertung des Libeskind-Baus als "Erinnerungsort" an die Vernichtung wie auch an

jüdisches Leben in Berlin, als "Bedeutungsträger" von Geschichte sowie als "Holocaust-Mahnmal"

3. There was a virtual media storm at the time. For one informative illustration, see Hoffmann-Axthelm 1997.

4. "Wenn Sie mich gerufen hätten, bevor Sie dieses Gebäude gebaut hätten, dann hätte ich eventuell versucht, mit Daniel Libeskind zu verhandeln und es ein bisschen anders zu bauen." (Wortprotokoll des Ausschusses für Kulturelle Angelegenheiten, 9. Sitzung, 19. Juni 2000, Abgeordnetenhaus von Berlin, 14. Wahlperiode, in: Senatsverwaltung für Kultur, VAI, Jüdisches Museum Museumskonzept, S. 15.)

5. These insights were first published in Bishop Kendzia (2014).

Chapter 1

Focus of the Research and Methodological Approach

The Research Question

The issue I want to explore is how do young Germany-based visitors approach this memorial museum and the history and culture it displays? From the preface, it should be clear that my own positioning is crucial in situating this study, the material collected, the questions asked, and the conclusions drawn. The issue to address then is not if I am part of the study and therefore co-constitute the material and ideas I have about it, but rather how this constellation—myself—young visitors—museum, and all that surrounds it, informs and forms the study as a whole and in particular situations. This is a challenging endeavor, but one that I hope to adequately explore throughout the work. In some cases, however, it is more clearly visible than in others: such as what I chose to study, how I view the museum, and the questions I found worthy of contemplation. Consequently, I begin here with my own first impressions of the museum and show, from there, the direction I chose to follow. Before deciding on the specifics of the research question, so quite early in the process, I conducted a perception walk in the JMB,[1] and noted my impressions in a field diary.

Choreographed Remembrance: A Perception Walk through the JMB

As I approach the entrance to the museum, it is warm and the sun is shining. The two police officers standing by the curb and the large bold-print security sign, forbidding the stopping of vehicles outside the museum, are hard to miss. Still, the atmosphere outside the museum is relaxed. Several teenagers are sit-

ting on the warm stone of the railing, or lying on the pavement. They are chatting in a language I do not quite catch, but guess to be Scandinavian of some kind. They joke with one another, laugh; a cola is shared among the group.

Once inside and through security, I observe a good many young people congregating in groups, about to begin their visits. The chatter continues, although more hushed (again not in German). The two ushers at the top of the steps to the underground axes take the tickets. Here, the visit is meant to begin. The stairs lead down to the Axis of Continuity [see Figure 3.1]. Here visitors, among them a number of youths, quietly view the artifacts displayed inside glass-fronted cases built into the walls. There is virtually no talking here. A group of high school–aged teenagers is being given a tour in Italian. Their faces betray no specific emotion. They do not smile or laugh. A whispered comment is occasionally exchanged. The mood is somber, respectful. A turn takes us along the Axis of the Holocaust at the end of which is the Holocaust Tower (see Figure 3.2). Display cases, housing possessions of victims, and captions about their fate are here too embedded along the walls—very personal artifacts, very personal stories. An attendant staffs the door to the tower. After a short time, she opens the door to let a small number of people out. Only then are we, myself and a small group of other waiting visitors, among them two young men, I would estimate being aged about sixteen, ushered in. The room is dark, narrow, and high. There is silence. The boys feel the walls and then squeeze themselves, one after the other, into the narrowest corner of the room. They look up and make hushed comments to one another. Are they looking for a specific aesthetic experience, I wonder? Then the door is opened and we exit. The Italian group are about to come in. They are told by the tour guide to be silent in the tower: "Silencio!"

I double back and find myself in the Axis of Exile (see Figure 3.3). Here the floor slants upward. Quietly, teenagers look at the displays. One takes notes. A text directly at the exit to the Garden of Exile: "asks us to think about the disorientation that exile brings." The Italian-speaking group are sitting outside in the Garden of Exile (Figure 3.4). The tour guide puts questions to the group, and the discussion is animated, but still without smiles, and still hushed. It is indeed somewhat disorienting, this going first uphill, then down, then through the pillars. The feeling of unsteady ground beneath one's feet makes one tread carefully. It is a very directed experience. Although I am focusing specifically on the younger visitors, I cannot help but notice an older woman, aged perhaps between fifty and sixty, crying at one corner of the garden.

Walking back along the Axis of Continuity, this time toward the stairs that lead to the permanent exhibition, I am again struck by how choreographed the visit is. The visitor is compelled to begin the visit with the aesthetic-memorial sections just described. The rest of the museum as such, then is put into this context of Holocaust remembrance, even though the permanent exhibition space displays a range or artifacts from "Two Millennia of German Jewish History," as the caption on the wall tells us. This is sure to have consequences for the overall experience. It may not be feasible to separate the effect of the aesthetic-memorial sections from that of the exhibition sections, as the former are preludes to the latter, and as such, set the tone and become the context for the entire visit. I wonder if this memorial-museum distinction though is consciously perceived as such by the other visitors.

The mood in the permanent exhibition space is much more casual. A group of German schoolchildren (estimated ages: between six and eight) play under and around the Wish Tree (Figure 3.5). Some are laughing. Some climb up and down the stairs that entwine the tree. This goes on for several minutes until their teacher scolds them, telling them to come down and be quiet. Some small children watch a film about the diaspora, some seem interested, some bored. A young boy ducks in and out of the exhibition, handling some of the didactic display-drawers, which help to explain the artifacts housed behind glass.

Arrows along the floor direct the visitor through the exhibitions. I would estimate that 90 percent of the people I observed followed this given path. Clearly, the visitor is meant to experience the museum along a particular, defined route.

I come up to a section with many interactive gadgets. The younger viewers are especially interested in these, pushing buttons, picking up earphones, etc. Next, a group of German high school students listens to an instructor/guide within the section dedicated to the rise of National Socialism. They listen intently. The mood though is perceptively more relaxed than in the axes underground. They discuss points in a conversational tone, not so hushed. Their body language is more at ease. Some slouch. Some squat. My walk throughout the rest of the museum goes quickly as there are few visitors to be seen. The busiest parts of the museum, by far, during my walk, were the underground axes. Once outside, I observe more teenagers lounging outside, talking casually among themselves. Whether they are pre- or post-visit, I cannot tell. The police officers, cheerful, are still keeping guard. The sun is still shining.[2]

Based on these early visits to the museum and observations of visitors, certain questions occurred to me: what is the role of emotional engagement in this remarkable building? How does it work as a memorial? Or as a museum? Or both? The working title of the study was then "The Jewish Museum Berlin: Memorial, Museum, Forum?" I thought it important not only to ask people what they felt and thought, but also crucially, to observe what they did. How do they carry out their visits?

Methodological Approach

These sorts of how questions, and the tools required to address them, convinced me early on to carry out this study within European ethnology. I needed to work with the tools of empirical field research to see and explore the "how." Further, reflexivity—the examination of one's own position including how one is positioned by the participants in the study—is given central placement within European ethnology. This is a point that I found crucial from the onset, not as something to be overcome (as all research is necessarily positioned and the readings always partial) but rather as something to be made visible, given space, and explored as data proper.[3] This endeavor may well involve a danger of falling into a trap of intellectual narcissism, but I would argue that self-reflexivity is necessary, not for its own sake, but rather as when and how it pertains to the material (or data) and analyses in the study.[4] In other words, I need to think and write about "me" when it is relevant to the research situation generally and to how the participants perform "themselves," specifically.

I mentioned that I come out of a different scholarly tradition—that of history and museum studies. Indeed, in 2006 European ethnology was new to me. My main academic influences within museum studies came from the field of education. It was here that I became interested in the work of pragmatists like John Dewey.[5] Aesthetic experience and the primacy of interactionism then were at the back (or front even) of my mind as I began to approach the topic. This I think is visible in the text recounting my initial preoccupations in the museum. I was also influenced by colleagues of mine in other fields (most notably sociology), and it was here that I first became interested in grounded theory (GT; Glaser and Strauss 1967). When it came time to prepare my own study, it was to this more familiar territory that I also turned.

GT is widely recognized within the social sciences and is based on the idea that themes and categories should emerge from the empirical data,[6] rather than testing a pre-formed hypothesis.[7] This also entails a systematic approach to analyzing qualitative data in order to arrive at original theory or a basic social process that can be applied more generally.[8] Further, and fully applicable to my aims, GT has been aptly described by practitioners as beginning with a research situation, the researcher's task being to understand what is happening there, and how the players manage their roles (Dick 2005). This situational starting point is appropriate to ethnological research, which considers the museum, in this case, as a field site. Wolfgang Kaschuba reminds us "the theoretical and methodological considerations do not end when one enters the field site; on the contrary, it is here where they often really begin" (2006: 205).[9] He also notes that the planned methodology rather than being fixed, is taken as "a provisional working plan into the field, which can still be substantially modified there" (Kaschuba 2006: 205).[10] This approach informs both the collection and the analysis of the material. I developed my methodological tools and general research questions, as well as the specific questions I would later include in the questionnaires, only after several visits to the museum, during which I observed visitors over stretches of time.

I carried out research with senior high school students from seven Berlin area schools, three being in the former West and three in the former East, and one in a region of the former West with a majority population of Turkish background. The choice to seek out these specific schools was based on a number of factors. The East-West comparison presented itself to me as a possible source of variation since there were striking differences in how the Jewish topic had been handled by the two Germanys during the Cold War. In very simplified terms: the leadership in East Germany represented World War II as a battle against fascism, in which the anti-Fascists (German Communists and their Soviet allies) were victorious. Here, the Jewishness of victims was suppressed in favor of anti-fascist credentials. The West German government, in contrast, eager to be seen as a good ally of the Western powers, thematized the past in terms of institutionalized expressions of remorse and public attempts at *wiedergutmachen.* (This term is commonly used in discussions about responsibility for the Nazi past. It translates literally as "to make things good again").[11] With these issues in mind, I wanted to include students from both former East and West Berlin. I should point out though that generationally, they were all born around the time of the fall of the wall, so more precisely they indicated that they were children of former East or West Germans. It was important for me also to include participants, still in the mainstream school system, mostly with non-German backgrounds, also as a source of potential variation. These participants indeed have a stake, as residents of Berlin and in many cases also German citizens,[12] and in all cases present and future museum visitors, in how this topic is thematized.

Access to the Field

While on the one hand, initial access to the museum as a field site was very easy: since the museum is a public institution, I could visit it as often as I liked, observe, speak with staff and visitors informally, and take plenty of notes.[13] On the other hand, reaching the specific visitors in whom I was most interested posed a challenge. With this in mind, and after discussions with museum visitor research staff at the JMB and my colleagues, I endeavored to contact all the high schools in Berlin, with senior levels, to propose my project to them and ask if any of the history/political science teachers and students might be interested in taking part in this study. This was a long process, which initially was met with little success. I did not receive any replies to my letters after several weeks, and even after the regular follow-up calls, it seemed the principals to whom I first addressed the correspondence were far too busy to deal with this request. Letter post and contacting principals was clearly not the way to go. I should mention that for much of the organizational work I am very much indebted to my husband who was born and raised in West Berlin. In conversations on the problem of gaining access to the schools, he had mentioned his own senior political science teacher, whom he remembered as having been a very effective teacher, engaged in the topic. We decided to try to seek him out personally and ask his advice on how to find the interested teachers and students. It turned out that his former teacher was still teaching and could recommend colleagues of his (teachers and one principal), who would likely be interested in this project. This contact started the ball rolling. In addition, it became clear that one had to contact the teachers first and inform the principals afterward. Four of the seven sessions then were facilitated this way. This included:

1. A *Gesamtschule* (comprehensive school) in a region of what was once in the West, which could be considered a lower–middle class area (the general range of professions of the parents in this area ranged from clerks, health-care assistants, and other comparable positions).[14]
2. A *Gymnasium* (academic high school/grammar school) in a similar area in former West Berlin.
3. A *Gymnasium* in an area of the former West in a region that could be considered upper middle class. (In the specific school, the parents of the participants practiced professions such as teachers, historians, sociologists, and medical doctors.)
4. A *Gymnasium* in a comparable central city region of what had been East Berlin.

Direct letters and visits to heads of history/political science departments resulted in the sessions with the remaining schools:

5. A *Gymnasium* in a region of the former West with a mostly immigrant population of predominantly Turkish descent. This area also suffers from particularly high unemployment.

6. A *Gymnasium* in an upper–middle class region in an area that was once in the East.
7. A *Gesamtschule* in the former East with a lower–middle class population.

The regions of the city in which these schools were located then spanned different socioeconomic categories (from what might be termed lower–middle class to upper–middle class). Each session included a pre-visit questionnaire, participant observations while the students visited the JMB, a post-visit questionnaire, and a focus group interview lasting between forty-five and seventy-five minutes with each student group, with 128 respondents. The groups participating in this study are specific in that they are all high school students who might be likely to continue to be active in historical matters (perhaps as future teachers, museum staff, or "history workers" as such, and certainly as museum visitors) and thereby might influence the future of this field. With this in mind, the individual participants are all senior high school students, grades eleven to thirteen (ages sixteen to twenty), who are completing or plan to complete what is called the *Abitur*.[15] This qualification is a prerequisite for university entrance. The Berlin high school system is also complicated and even confusing at times. At the time my research began, it consisted of *Hauptschule* (lower secondary school from grade seven to ten), *Realschule* (middle secondary school from grade seven to ten), and *Gymnasium* (academic high school/grammar school from grade seven to thirteen). *Gymnasien* finish with the *Abitur*. This is the general higher education certificate that is a prerequisite for access to university or college (and now increasingly to many professional training programs). And finally, it includes the *Gesamtschule* (comprehensive school, a mix of all three types described above). Since then, the Berlin secondary school system has been reorganized, but not fundamentally reformed. *Hauptschule, Realschule,* and *Gesamtschule* have been merged into the *Integrierte Sekundarschule* (integrated secondary school), continuing the concept of the *Gesamtschule*. The *Gymnasium* finishes now with the *Abitur* exam after grade twelve, while those students at a *Sekundarschule* who are able to do the *Abitur* cannot do it before grade thirteen. (Note too that the school systems can vary in the different German federal lands.) Thus, the inequality of the structures are maintained, since the *Gymnasien* continue to operate, as such. Crucial to my study is the fact that attending school after grade ten is not a legal requirement. It is also after this point that the students aiming for the *Abitur* have more freedom in choosing basic core and elective courses. Further, the topic of the persecutions of the Jews under the Nazis is covered, albeit in varying degrees, across the curricula, in grade ten. Hence, all the students would have had some relatively recent school-based exposure to part of the topic relevant to the museum before being part of this project.

All of the groups were also from history or political science classes. Participation in this study was voluntary and relied on the students and teachers' willingness to give their time and active input. In addition, the teachers who agreed to take part were committed to incorporating the JMB within their curricula.

Multifaceted Methodology

Explicit methodological triangulation, that is the use of more than one method to explore a phenomenon as in Norman Denzin (1970), is important. An appreciation of the need for methodologies that have depth and scope has been voiced recently in reviews of museum visitor studies. Eilean Hooper-Greenhill notes that since there has been a shift to understanding that "meaning making processes are contingent, variable and fluid," there is a need for a turn to "interpretive philosophies and qualitative research methods" in museum visitor studies (2006: 373). Sharon Macdonald's study of the Science Museum in London, an ethnography with a combination of methodologies, has made valuable contributions to the field and informs my own work. Macdonald's methodological approach is essential "to understand how visitors culturally framed their experience" (2002: 219). Eric Gable (2010) also notes that ethnography can offer much to museum studies. He emphasizes the importance of combining research methods: close observation of visitors in situ, open-ended interviews coupled with questionnaires that build on interferences and queries based on these. Gable too, referring to and critical of the broad literature on visitor studies, shares Hooper-Greenhill's argument. He stresses ethnographic approaches that focus on what visitors actually do at museums, rather than merely concern themselves with how many enter the door, or whether they can answer correctly on a questionnaire what they have seen and learned, or worse, whether or not they have enjoyed themselves, will be a major improvement (Gable 2010: 110). It is my hope that this present study can also contribute to such an "improvement."

My research goals also have a lot in common with those suggested by Erkki Huhtamo. He calls his approach "exhibition anthropology" in which the museum is conceived of as "A kind of experience apparatus—a combination of material features, social roles, and institutional practices and policies that provide a framework for visitors' experiences. Understood as an apparatus, the museum is a system of anticipation and regulations that visitors are supposed to follow" (Huhtamo 2015: 272).

Indeed, implicit norms and regulations—that later became visible through the research at the JMB—are central to grappling with the larger social issues that form and inform the culture of memory in Germany. This present study then, much like Huhtamo's work, aims to pay close attention to "patterns of use, and also reflect on their wider theoretical and cultural underpinnings" (Huhtamo 2015: 273).

The central positioning of the tool: participant observation with its implicit triangulation is also crucial to my endeavor as it entails a number of methods in itself. One not only observes, but also interacts and can ask questions at the time (cf. Flick 2009: 309–10). As a participant observer, the researcher interacts with the subjects of research and the field, considers all this, and is continually adjusting the questioning and the theoretical relevance, as the experiences in the field require. This is also important in order to avoid focusing on not only what people say but, crucially, what people do. I used the pre-visit questionnaires primarily as an exploratory tool in order to ascertain specific information about the backgrounds of the visitors, previous knowledge on, and feelings about the topic. The post-visit questionnaires served to gather their immediate impressions of the JMB. All the questions were open. I opted for open questions in order to try to avoid pre-guessing or limiting the replies, as much as this is possible. While this makes the analysis difficult, I reasoned that this was worth the challenge. Further, I knew that this was not to be a random sampling quantitative study. I had no intention of submitting the replies to statistical significance tests, for example. I found it, therefore, preferable to allow for a maximum range of potential replies in all cases. This is also appropriate to the exploratory purpose of the questionnaires and to the space that I wanted to leave the respondents to narrate as they wished. This was indeed fruitful in that very many answers that I would never have predicted came up.[16]

The observations made during the visits and, to a more limited extent, the questionnaire replies, then informed the group interviews, which allowed for a deepened contextualization of the observations. I opted for group interviews in order to maintain something of the group effect and dynamic of the visits. It made sense then to have the students discuss them not only with me, but also with each other in a conversational and interactive manner. Ralf Bohnsack touched on this value of group interviews, noting that: "Shared experience is indeed most comprehensively *articulated* there where those who shared it congregate" (Emphasis in the original; Bohnsack 2009: 377).[17]

The order of events in setting up and carrying out the research sessions were, with minor variations, as follows: once a teacher had indicated interest, I would visit the class, describe the project, and obtain the consent of the students. This was an important step, not just ethically, but also in order to gage the interest of the participants. Then, provided the students agreed, a date would be set for the museum visit. There was one occasion when a teacher expressed interest, but after several weeks of back and forth phone calls, he confessed that he just could not find an "appropriate" class to participate. Interestingly, this was in a school from a part of former East Berlin known for neo-Nazi activity. On the day of the visit, I would meet the students and teacher beforehand and have them fill out the pre-visit questionnaire. In all but one case, the questionnaires were filled out shortly before the visit to the museum. Next, the students and I would visit the museum together. On three occasions, the teachers were present at the beginning and end of the visit but did not remain with the groups in the museum. One teacher remained with his group for the majority of the visit. His explanation for this is indeed telling and will be explored in some depth. During three visits, the teachers were not present. There were no guided tours, but it did happen on occasion that a group of students would find a guide and eavesdrop on a part of a tour. After the visits, I would have the students fill in the post-visit questionnaire. A few days later, I would come back to the classroom and conduct the group interview. On the first two visits, however, the interview took place directly in the museum after the visit. I found this was exhausting for the students and not particularly productive and decided to arrange it differently. On all but one occasion, the teachers were present during these interviews. I would enter the classroom and ask questions based on what I observed during the visit and to some extent on questionnaire replies, especially when these held replies that I found puzzling or particularly noteworthy. What followed were discussions on the topic with me and with each other in the classroom. Further, I could not conduct a group interview with one of the groups, as the schedules of the students could not accommodate one. This group rather spent several hours in the museum with me, during which there were many interactions and discussions at the time. In this case then, the intimate nature of the participant observations allowed for a lot of implicit triangulation as I could ask about and explore in some detail specifics in the museum as they arose.

The multifaceted methodology facilitated an exploration of the factors that might influence and interact with the varying ways in which the visitors behaved in the museum. Hence, the illustration of certain themes could have depth, since statements about the visitors' previous positioning and the observed behavior in the museum, as well as follow-up articulations and clarifications are at hand. This aids in situating and integrating the results. This is by no means the complete picture, as it were. It is, however, one with a certain scope that might allow for new insights. For example, at times the observed behavior in the museum seemed to be in contradiction to written (perhaps socially desirable?) replies. This could then be explored in the interviews. It is in this way that I applied theoretical sampling on an ongoing basis. I could and did ask new questions of participants and the materials, based on the ideas that came up during the museum visits and during the ongoing analysis process. Further, this combination of tools was valuable in that the anonymous questionnaires at times contained/facilitated statements (controversial or derogatory) and longer individual narrations that did not come up in the other group settings. What I could not realistically manage, however, was to seek out yet more new participants. I am not sure that this is essential for this project, since 128 is already a large number and so many variations did come up even within and among the groups. Still, it would, I think, be a worthy and valid pursuit to survey visitors with other stated interests, perhaps not on the university entrance track, or even to go specifically to the one Jewish high school in Berlin, to explore yet more potential variations.

It was this combination of materials that helped me, for example, to build a *basic social process* that I found could facilitate the telling of a coherent story. In line with GT techniques (Strauss and Corbin 1990), I began first by coding (putting down ideas about) the questionnaire replies, interviews, and observations in an open, brainstorming fashion. Then I proceeded to undertake a constant comparison of the ideas, cross-referencing them with each other, looking for correlations and potential causes. In this way I built a basic social process, which in very brief terms goes something like this: "If the visitor attests pre-visit position x, she/he tends to behave in the museum in way y and talk/write about the visit in terms z." In many cases, straight lines (correlations) could be drawn, and potential causality might even be inferred, but certainly not "proven" as such. While this is part of the story and plausible, it was certainly not the whole story, and limiting myself to it rigidly obscured two crucial points: first, it did not do justice to the complexity of the field and the variations within those groups who might have attested similar pre-visit positions and post-visit articulations. Second, it did not allow sufficient room for reflexivity. My position, which is central to contextualizing the interactions, was hardly visible within this basic social process.

In order to get fresh ideas about the materials, I presented a lot of material and a little bit of analysis at several international conferences, and discussed my concerns with my colleagues. The reactions, although mostly very positive, and my own reflections over time, lead me to be convinced that in order to avoid oversimplification and inadvertently reinforcing essentialist ideas, I needed to start with the situations in the field. I then proceeded to analyze these first in order to show the complexity and even seeming contradictions that were visible there, but not nearly as visible in the plot of my basic social process. Further, the categories that I found and gave names to did not seem very original in content to me. They had much in common with concepts I had before become acquainted with (Connerton: bodily memory; Hirsch: post memory; Young: collected memories) or since (Bourdieu: habitus; Halbwachs: collective memory). In addition, I was only comfortable taking the abstractions so far before I felt that the material behind them disappeared. I, therefore, turned to Adele Clarke's (2005) contribution *Situational Analysis: Grounded Theory after the Postmodern Turn.* Had I been perhaps a more experienced practitioner of GT (this is the first project in which I have actively used the techniques), I might have come to this point sooner. Still, I am convinced that the experience of open and axial coding, building conditional matrices, finding problems, and deciding and being convinced independently that the empirical material was really too varied and complicated to allow for a rigid traditional application of GT, was essential to my learning process. It was encouraging and thought provoking to subsequently read Clarke's contribution, which echoed and addressed many of the concerns with which I was struggling. Namely, focusing empirically on the situation as a whole was crucial (Clarke 2005: 66). For me this corresponded to starting with the situations as such (in and with the museum, during the interviews, and other interactions), as a whole with all the inherent variability. Clarke's call for enhanced reflexivity throughout her book (cf. Clarke 2005: 12–15, 17–18) also gelled well with the importance of the researcher's own position, which is a major factor in my study and within European ethnology generally. I was also appreciative of Clarke's assertion that one does not, necessarily, have to create substantive or formal theory, but that "more modest and partial but serious, useful, and hopefully provocative grounded analyses, sensitizing concepts, analytics and theorizing are adequate" (Clarke 2005: 29). In addition, important for my work, Clarke further stressed the applicability of GT approaches across disciplines (2005: 4).

A shift of focus to the "messy" situations does not mean for me that I am abandoning the basic social process, but rather that I am not starting with it, or insisting on a dogmatic or rigid alignment with it. It is part of the story I am telling, but it is not the only or whole story that I feel compelled to recount. The GT approach has been invaluable to me from the onset. It has allowed me to do two things, which have been crucial to this endeavor: first, the constant comparison method helped me not to panic in the early stages of the empirical material gathering, when strange and unexpected results came up. This was especially helpful when I started to see variations upon variations emerging. One of the problems that I had with the concept of building theory out of data was an underlying assumption, I perceived, that the data is just out there. While the term "emerge" is useful, it needs to be qualified. In the research situation, I, as the researcher, co-constitute the material in that I call it up in the questions I ask, in the priority I give, and so on. At times, it seems that the term "emerge" denotes an organic-like process seemingly independent of the researcher or data collector. The reality I see is rather co-constructed by the assumptions (conscious and unconscious) I bring to the situation. This, of course, is true for all researchers. We are always positioned. The issue I want to explore though is the how of it and to address it throughout the project rather than push it to the margins as if it is something that can be overcome. Had I insisted upon a rigid question or hypothesis, I might have been tempted to ignore or discard what I perceived as seeming contradictions. Rather than do this, I struggled with these findings, continuing to compare the categories with each other and think about them. Here is just one example to illustrate briefly: many of the visitors who attested a high level of prior interest and previous knowledge on the subject of Jewish history behaved in ways that indicated boredom in the museum, while many of those who indicated no interest behaved in ways that indicated interest rather than boredom. How to make sense of this? In the early stages, this seemed counterintuitive, but throughout the coding process, and focusing on the situation and the positioning of the visitors, it became clearer that what was meant by "interest" was not the same to all participants in practice. The specific episodes that led to this finding are explored in Chapter 4.

Second, remaining in and asking new questions of the empirical material in turn allowed me to be inspired by it and have new ideas and go in unexpected directions, while still being precise, thorough, and systematic. This, in practice, meant that I could adjust my research question even well into the fieldwork. This is indeed what happened. Originally, I had been more concerned with the dichotomy—memorial versus museum, corresponding to underground versus upper floors—that I myself saw in the museum, as well as issues of emotional engagement as a pedagogical principle. In reviewing the variety of the questionnaire replies and interviews, the topic of the museum as a site of political education, a sort of moral site, as expressed by many of the visitors themselves, came to the forefront. Here is an example to illustrate. During one group interview, the conversation had moved from being impressed with the architecture of the museum to being made to feel guilty, specifically in the Menashe Kadishman installation entitled *Fallen Leaves*. Here a long section of the room is covered with metal mask-like structures (see Figure 3.6). The sign beside it invited visitors to walk over the installation noting that it was to commemorate "not only the victims of the Nazis but victims of violence everywhere" (Field diary 10 September 2007). Here are excerpts from the group interview:

> [A young woman explains]: What I found pretty cruel was that one did not have the opportunity … I mean, one had the opportunity to demean the people, if I interpret it this way, by walking over the faces, so one had no opportunity at all to do something nice for them or to express one's sympathy. One could only … so I found that a bit guilt inducing. (Transcript, hereafter refers as TR, 3 group interview 13 September 2007: 3)

> [One of her male classmates adds]: I must say that we did not live through all that and that it [the Nazi time] has been narrated to us and, in the end, we are not responsible. And yet, what is passed on to us from our parents, from the entire society, is that one has to tackle this topic, that one will still try to prevent any right-wing activities, that one really very strongly, we as Germans, we who have this history behind us, must fight against this. When one then sees the victims of that history, as mentioned, the Jews there in this museum, one does get a bit the feeling of guilt and shame because our ancestors were largely guilty of what happened then. (TR, 3 group interview 13 September 2007: 3)

> [Another young man agrees]: Yes, since the main events happened over sixty years ago—one should also keep this in mind—it is that we actually have no practical connection, except maybe our grandparents—in my case is it especially my grandfather, where the only real and truly tangible connection is—who somehow know something about that time, who lived through it. He was also seriously injured, almost died, and so on. In any event, there is no longer a real connection. Like Frank has already said,[18] we only know about this from stories told to us by people we know: our parents, relatives, friends, and acquaintances, and from books. As a result, it is also interesting to experience something, to roughly put oneself a bit in that position. (TR, 3 group interview 13 September 2007: 3)

From these sorts of exchanges, it became clear to me that for many of the participants the museum visits and research situations were taking place or better said being performed within a context of political education; hence the move to focus on this concept. Mentions of guilt, shame, and moral/political responsibility did come up well before this interview on the questionnaires, for example. Indeed, this exchange was preceded by my asking about the replies on the questionnaires, which indicated guilt feelings.

Here we see how my question ("What feelings do you personally associate with Jewish history in Germany?") then co-constitute the material. This question had, in turn, been a result of the behavior I had seen in many previous visits to the museum, not to mention the myriad of media reports and public events that used emotional language to discuss this topic. These issues then did not come up, or emerge, out of thin air. The discussions in the groups facilitated a back and forth dialogue, as well as some in-depth handling and articulation. The range of replies helps to make the variety and complexity of the situations visible.

In the passages above, these young visitors positioned their approach to the JMB as relating to what it means to be "German" and to contemplate this past in terms of political responsibility/action—to fight against right-wing extremism, for example. This they tied significantly to memory (passed down either directly via grandparents and/or collectively by society) of the Nazi past. This is not to say that the memorial/museum issue and emotional responses are not addressed. On the contrary, emotional expressions too are present (feelings of guilt and sadness, for example), while on several occasions the striking difference between the underground axes (with their memorial connotations) and the colorful, more pleasant upper floors was indeed thematized and is explored in the analyses. However, these particular elements did not capture adequately what was going on in and around the museum, and in and around the research sessions, especially in terms of performance, identification, my own role in the research, and often conflicting readings of museum elements and situations. These configurations are explored in detail in Chapter 3 and beyond. First, however, and because of the centrality of political education and memory, it is to this question of context that I now turn: where and how does this study—and the JMB—fit in the broader field of memory studies and political education?

Notes

1. The term "conversation walk" is also common, but I find my literal translation of the German term *Wahrnehmungsspaziergang* more appropriate here.
2. The text is based on field notes taken in May 2006.
3. Cf. Clarke 2005: esp. xxvii, 12–13; Lindner 1981: 52–53.
4. Cf. Clarke 2005: 13.
5. Seminal works, which had a significant influence on my thought, are Dewey 1938 and 1934.
6. This is especially true in Anglo-Saxon social sciences, and although it is less widely spread in Germany, it has become a firm part of "methodological discourse" (Hildenbrand 2009: 41).

7. I share Clarke's (2005) understanding that researchers are always influenced by prior knowledge before beginning an empirical project. Moreover, this prior knowledge is essential to deciding which questions to explore. Clarke repeats the point, and I concur, that: "There is actually 'something ludicrous about pretending to be a theoretical virgin' (Robert Loescher, quoted in Elkins 2003: 31)" (Clarke 2005: 13). I have tried to make my positioning explicit above, and although I did not set out to prove a particular hypothesis as such, prior knowledge and a literature review were essential to the choices I made, for example in selecting the groups that I wanted to survey.

8. This is a contested point, especially given the reflexivity called for, and I explain my adapted use as it arose and turn to situational analysis (as in Clarke 2005) later in this chapter.

9. Dass die theoretische und methodische Klärungsarbeit mit dem Eintritt ins Feld nicht abgeschlossen ist, sondern hier oft erst richtig beginnt.

10. Ein vorläufiges Arbeitsprogramm mit ins Feld, das dort noch wesentlich modizifiert werden kann.

11. This simplified explanation only outlines the broad differences and can by no means do justice to the shades and variations. A few key sources that go into depth are Fullbrook 2002; Herf 1997; Koonz 1994; Ostow 1996, 2001.

12. German citizenship law underwent a paradigm shift in 2000, which allowed children born in Germany to non-German parents after 1990 to be legally eligible for citizenship. The law itself was enacted in 2004. This is the shift to "acquisition by place of birth (*jus solis*)" (Mushaben 2008: 33). A number of the participants in my study fall into this category and have taken out German citizenship. Up until very recently, these individuals were expected to choose between German nationality and that of their parents later in life. This was a "conditional *jus soli* [for] children born in Germany to legal foreign residents; options to become a German citizen or to remain German by renouncing other nationalities between the age of eighteen and twenty-three" (Mushaben 2008: 33). While other participants were children (who also fall into the problematic and opaque category of residents of migrant background) of at least one German parent, and had access to German citizenship automatically according to the legal basis of acquisition "by birth (*jus sanguinis*)" (Mushaben 2008: 32), which has obtained since 1949 and does still apply. The implications of these categories for the self-identification and descriptions by the participants in this study are explored in detail in the chapters that follow. The citizenship law is naturally far more complex than given here, and its application and practices can vary widely from federal land to federal land.

13. I should point out that even in informal conversations with staff, I did inform them that I was carrying out a study and might include details, anonymously, in publications.

14. These class distinctions can be problematic if one wants to stick dogmatically to them. I use them more as descriptives again here to give a general impression of the areas of the city involved.

15. This is roughly equivalent to the British A-levels or in Ontario, Canada, the OACs, for example.
16. For further discussion on my use of the questionnaires and an English version of the questionnaire that I constructed, see Appendix A. For further discussion of the value of open versus closed questions see, for example: Converse and Presser 1986: 33–34; Foddy 1993: 151–52; and Schuman and Presser 1981: 7–10.
17. Allerdings wird gemeinsames Erleben dort am Umfassendsten zur *Artikulation* gebracht, wo diejenigen sich zusammenfinden, denen dieses gemeinsam ist.
18. Unless otherwise stated, all names are pseudonyms.

Chapter 2

Memory, Political Education, and the Positioning of the JMB

From Memory to Remembrance, to Past Presencing

> I have begun to remember more and more often my visits to Holocaust memorials … that invite me to remember events I never experienced directly. Indeed, the further the Holocaust recedes in time, the more prominent its memorials and museums become. (Young 1994: 19)

These words by Holocaust Memorial expert James Young resonate with me personally and form the basis of an understanding of memory that underlies this work. Like Young, like myself, the visitors in this study are interacting with a site of memory dedicated to events that occurred long before they were born. This temporal distance is crucial to approaching the sort of remembrance that is at play. Young also notes that

> The reasons for Holocaust memorials and the kinds of memory they generate vary as widely as the sites themselves. Some are built in response to traditional Jewish injunctions to remember, others according to a government's need to explain a nation's past to itself. Where the aim of some memorials is to educate the next generation and to inculcate in it a sense of shared destiny, other memorials are intended to attract tourists. (1994: 19)

The variations in visitor experience that are explored in the chapters that follow confirm Young's assessment, while also qualifying it. Rather than generate memory as such, from my reading of the situations in the museum, the JMB offers an opportunity for visitors to participate in a memorial activity. Such opportunities are variously taken up—or not. Here Wulf Kansteiner's take on the topic is crucial. He recommends that researchers

> conceptualize collective memory as the result of the interaction among three types of historical factors: the intellectual and cultural traditions that frame all our representations of the past, the memory makers, who selectively adopt and manipulate

these traditions and the memory consumers who use, ignore, or transform such artefacts according to their own interests. (Kansteiner 2002: 180)

This approach, which focuses on interaction, and aims to avoid the pitfalls of pseudo-psychoanalytic assumptions and categories, has become central to my analysis. Further, the JMB, rather than having one clear goal, presents many at once, some of which seem paradoxical. The tensions between such goals—such as "not being a Holocaust museum" and yet marking this event with its evocative architecture—play out on the ground and impact visitor experience.

A great deal has, of course, been written on the topic of memory from many fields. An overview of this would be neither helpful in approaching the ethnographic material nor particularly relevant to it. A few key concepts are worthy of clarification here. A Halbwachsian idea of memory as socially constructed is applicable, but only to a point. Maurice Halbwachs's main thesis is that memory is a construct, which functions in collective contexts and which can be evoked selectively.[1] This concept envisions memory, however, as something possessed, albeit intangibly, and then shared. This does not seem to apply to much of the material relating to the young men and women who partook in my study. Another scholar, whose work on the topic of memory, especially in terms of recalling the Nazi era in Germany, also has relevance for this study is Aleida Assmann. Her descriptions of various definitions of memory are coherent and intelligent. For example, her description of "communicative memory" appears to apply to the statements of some of the young visitors included at the end of the previous chapter. Those very statements caused me to rethink my research question and include political education as a key component.[2] Assmann notes the importance of the family in this as a decisive communicative-memory-forming social unit:

> Through narrating, listening, enquiring and further telling, the radius of one's own memories increases. Children and grandchildren incorporate a part of the memories of their older relatives into their own memorial account where that which is actually experienced and that which is heard intersect. (Assmann 2006: 25–26)[3]

This indeed seems to be the case at the individual level. However, it is the jump to terms such as collective or national memory that seems problematic and does not help me to approach the variety of approaches visible in the ethnographic material. Assmann outlines and analyzes top-down examples of monuments and memorials, books, and media events. These are all constructs of the milieu to which she also belongs, a socio-intellectual elite one. From this, she posits a more or less shared cultural memory. She refers repeatedly to such products as instances of "shared memory/remembering" (Assmann 2006: 107) and "a collective memory of the Germans" (198).[4]

I have come to understand and share the exasperation I perceived in Jay Winter's tone at a conference I attended in 2008 in Kent entitled (fittingly), "Cultural Memory." As a prelude to his keynote speech, he made the following emphatic statement: *"Nations don't remember! People do!"* By conflating a cultural/national memory as such with examples of elite political discourse *about* memory of the past, one can occlude variation and too easily slip into oversimplifying monolithic generalizations.

It is the imprecise use of the terminology that has me confused and frustrated. This entity that Assmann calls "shared memory" looks very different from below. From my own outside and on the ground perspective with the visitors to the museum, who come from various walks of life, origins, and social classes, this entity looks much more like a dominant political discourse/culture. The museums, books, films, and the like are products of this narrative. They do not embody any shared memory *per se*. Indeed, I do not perceive such broadly shared memory at all. In reviewing the variations in the ethnographic material from groups of visitors, one might have expected to be somewhat similar (all Berlin-based, senior high school history students, who are completing the *Abitur,* and who volunteered to take part in the study); I find myself coming back to James Clifford in his assertion that "few communities, even the most 'local,' are homogeneous" (Clifford 1997: 208). I also recall Wolfgang Kaschuba's comments precisely on the topic of a shared memory of National Socialism:

> The relevant historical museums and exhibitions continue to boom, so that the aura of the dark German past still appears to be effective. … If historical consciousness is substantially based on "shared remembering," on the existence of particular moral, cultural conventions of the shared responsibility for history, then there is the need in each society for clear political encouragement and guidelines. A societal understanding about this has to be continually re- and newly negotiated. (Kaschuba 2005: 184)[5]

He continues to assert that:

> The lapses of the early [post World War II] years cannot be simply repaired, since neither the reasons nor the memories were really made into a collective matter … Only if the times and the rituals, if the voices and the places are both officially legitimized and multi-vocal and thick enough, do they actually function as an "archive of collective memory." We hardly have access to any such "archive" of memory about German history during National Socialism. (Kaschuba 2005: 196)[6]

In other words, while Kaschuba notes that the relevant museums seem to be effective, he goes on to cast serious doubt on the presence of an actually shared memory on the topic. An actual source that would feed an authentic memory of this time was simply not available. If this is the case, I need to ask, what is it then that the young visitors are tapping into?

The distinction in wording (i.e. my preference for calling the products of memory makers a *dominant discourse*) is important for my study for two reasons. First, calling the "memory" a dominant discourse in this case helps to make the power relations and asymmetries more visible. This is key to interpreting how visitors approached the museum. Some fully partook of this discourse and performed their visits accordingly. Some did not, seemingly unaware of the expectation that they do this. Some openly and provocatively opposed the expectations. This led to conflicts with the museum staff, other visitors, and even fellow classmates and teachers. Approaching the museum as a field within a coded discursive system is much more precise and helps in analyzing the situations as they arose.

Second, and arguably even more important, is the message that using the terms like "shared memory" to describe a collection of discursive products might send out to those who find themselves outside of aspects of the prevailing narrative. (I have come to include myself in this category.) This may well be an unintended message, but it comes across to me, as it seems to as well to many of the participants in my study, who also found themselves on the outside. The message is broadly (and perhaps too bluntly put) as follows: "This is our national memory: if you do not share it or perform it as we do, you are not part of our collective." A dominant narrative or even a specific, preferred form of collective memory, if one insists on keeping the term, unlike an assumed "shared memory," is much more open to appropriation, redefinition, and subversion, while not necessarily excluding anyone from a given collective. Jackie Feldman's work, an ethnography of Israeli youth voyages to Poland, for example, shows the spaces where such subversion can take place. He too sees a dominant narrative—he refers to a "particular collective memory" being promoted (Feldman 2008: 10) and proceeds to empirically demonstrate a varied and nuanced partaking and performance thereof.

Karen E. Till (2005) also touches on the problem of exclusion that concerns me. This is thrown into sharp relief in the following excerpt of an interview with Christine Fischer-Defoy, Active Museum president,[7] about the then plans for the Topography of Terror exhibition on the site where the Nazi Gestapo leadership held its offices. Karen Till (KT) asks:

Why is this separation [between victim and perpetrator] so important?

Christine Fischer-Defoy (CFD): Maybe because the commemoration of the victims would divert attention away from the perpetrators. The responsibility is so important for us—to keep an awareness of the perpetrators in the city and to deal with the people who did it. For German politicians, as well as for the German public, it is "easier" to identify with the victims than to deal with fact that their grandparents were perpetrators. When you mix the educational work about the history of the perpetrators with the commemoration of the victims, it becomes the "Kohl politics" of "we are all so sad, and let us forget that we were the criminals who did it."

KT: When you make such a distinction between the places of the victims and the places of the perpetrators, does that mean that Jews or Sinti and Roma will never be seen as Germans? ...

CFD: They are Germans as well. It is important that we are the country of the perpetrators and the country of the victims as well—Germans were also victims. (Till 2005: 128)

The difficulty that Christine Fischer-Defoy has in addressing Karen Till's question is evident. She has taken the essentialness of the category German equals perpetrator so for granted that she seems to get thrown off track and tries to go back on her original argument. It is also interesting that she uses the terms "we" to refer to the Nazi criminals, although she clearly was not an actual perpetrator. It is her "Germanness" that causes her to use this pronoun. The mechanism of exclusion, however unintended it may be, is made explicit here. If political education is about taking responsibility for the "German" past, within a frame that draws such hard and taken-for-granted boundaries between perpetrators (and their descendants) and victims, then what room remains for multi-vocality? What impact does such a fixed idea of Germanness have on descendants of migrants, who cannot claim a form of belonging based on past perpetratorhood? What are the implications for integration—finding a way to belong here?

To engage with such questions, in terms of how the museum is perceived, I find it more productive to turn to the performative aspects of memory as they are embodied in the acts of the visitors (not only written, but also gestural, and bodily). Indeed, it is in and through interaction of people with objects of memory (museums, archives, films, memorials, memorial days, other people, etc.) that memory is, in fact, formed. And this enacted memory is necessarily performative. This aspect of museum *visiting* and Holocaust *remembering* as a social practice is a key point and helps to shed light on many of the situations that arose in my research. Returning to James Young's contributions, one of his stated aims (and one I have come to share adamantly) is "to break down the notion of any memorial's 'collective memory' altogether. Instead, I prefer to examine 'collected memory' ... If societies remember, it is only insofar as their institutions and rituals organize, shape, even inspire their constituents' memories. For a society's memory cannot exist outside of those people who do the remembering" (Young 1993: xi). This approach helps, I think, in the endeavor to avoid conflating products of a memorial discourse with actual memory in individuals or groups for that matter. What groups do together may well be visit a museum and behave in a similar manner. What they might actually remember of the narratives being memorialized, other than this visit itself and habitus memory (i.e. how to behave in line with the occasion, cf. Goffman 1963) derived from such visits, is not necessarily common at all.

I am also attracted to Jay Winter's work, which favors the term remembrance, and sees collective memory as

> A matrix of interwoven individual memories. It has no existence without them, but the components of individual memory intersect and create a kind of pattern with an existence of its own … To change metaphors, it is possible to speak of collective memory as … a sort of choir singing, or better still, a sing-along. This kind of event which is not very regimented, and in which each participant begins singing at a different time and using a somewhat different text or melody but done according to norms … accepted by other members of that informal choir. (Winter and Sivan 1999: 28)

This choir metaphor is helpful as we can see what happens when some sing out of key, or if several choirs converge and come into conflict in the same space. Further one can ask: who conducts the choir, as such, who knows the songs? What does the predominant repertoire sound like? These issues come up at length in the chapters that follow. Still, here is a brief look into the framing of how a chorus of German visitors might be expected to perform.

> I was discussing my results with a high school history teacher who had heard about my work through a mutual friend. I mentioned particular visiting practices, ranging from expressions of solemn dismay (*Betroffenheit*), to complaints of being made to feel guilty and emotionally manipulated by the sad stories of what "we had done to the Jews." (Here the taken-for-grantedness of "German" as the dominant national *ethnos* is again visible.) The teacher indicated that she was not at all surprised by these statements and related the following to me. She had been to the Jewish Museum Berlin with a group of her students, also middle-class Berliners of West German background, and some had evidently written some complaining remarks, not unlike the ones I mentioned to her, in the guest book. Somehow (exactly how she did not know), these comments were traced back to her class. As a result, she and the other history teachers were called to account before the principal who admonished them, telling them to better educate their students.[8]

This is an illustrative example of an attempt to control the behavior of a group of visitors. The teacher was supposed to conduct her group properly, when she failed to do so, her superior held her responsible. It is likely that the school principal feared such comments might reflect badly on his school.[9] Irit Dekel has also observed similar situations at the Holocaust Memorial in which guides stated that any utterances they interpreted to be anti-Semitic could not be tolerated there (Dekel 2013: 34). In this case then, the guides would be leading the choir, as such.

Further, I share Winter's preference for the term "collective remembrance" as it highlights performance. Remembrance is something done, more or less ritually, depending on context as opposed to something possessed. Thus, it avoids psychological assumptions about fixed internal states, which are at once unmeasurable in my view and furthermore beside the point. This insistence on believing to describe internal states (emotional or otherwise) is a weakness of the concepts of memory relied on by many scholars in this field. The term memory, however, is so prevalent in my field of study that I hesitate to drop it altogether.

Unlike the term memory, remembrance revolves around something done together as a group. It does not assume that corresponding images are present in the mind of individuals. Sharon Macdonald's (2012) contribution "past presencing," which focuses on the ways in which people make an imagined past present is also particularly helpful and applicable to the material gathered in this study.

The chapters that follow then are also an endeavor to counterbalance the vast literature on memory, based almost exclusively on studies of cultural products and their makers, with an in-depth study of actual receptions of such products. This is indeed crucial in trying to question problematic normative assumptions that intended messages are actually those received by consuming publics. In other words, as Wulf Kansteiner has called for, this study is one, which tries to "link facts of representation with facts of reception" (Kansteiner 2002: 179).

Museums and Political Education

A long-standing connection between modern public museums and political education in a broader sense is well established. Tony Bennett articulates this concisely. He describes such museums as

> institutions … adapted to the development of new forms of civic self-understanding. … [They are] above all else governmental and civic … and their publicness …

> has been, and continues to be, shaped by their interactions with other civic and governmental institutions whose development has been coeval with their own—libraries, adult education, and, above all, mass schooling—and shaped by broader governmental articulations of the relations of culture and *citizenship*. (emphasis mine; Bennett 2006: 48)

Such global frameworks should be kept in mind. Richard Sandell, for example, notes that

> In recent years, museums have become increasingly confident in proclaiming their value as agents of social change and, in particular, articulating their capacity to promote cross-cultural understanding, to tackle prejudice and intolerance and to foster respect for difference. (Sandell 2007: 2)

The American Association of Museums, also (cited in Sandell 2007) clearly expresses such goals:

> Museums perform their most fruitful public service by providing an educational experience in the broadest sense: by fostering the ability to live in a pluralistic society and to contribute to the resolution of challenges we face as global citizens … Museums can no longer confine themselves simply to preservation, scholarship, and exhibition. … They must recognize that the public dimension of museums leads them to perform the public service of education. (Sandell 2007: 2)

The global appeal of the Holocaust as a prime locus for remembrance is highlighted by Daniel Levy and Natan Sznaider. They argue that the explosion of Holocaust historiography and commemoration over the last twenty years is a result of "the need for a moral touchstone in an age of uncertainty" (Levy and Sznaider 2002: 93). The Holocaust is something that can be universally condemned, mourned, and applied to the present, albeit within each unique national context. The authors refer to "the duality of memory: the memories of the Holocaust came to be regarded as unique with reference to the past and universal for the future. That is to say, the Holocaust past is something that happened primarily to the Jews, while the Holocaust future might happen to anyone" (Levy and Sznaider 2002: 96). Naturally, the types of and specific expectations for such "citizenship" mentioned by Bennett above or "global citizens" alluded to by the American Association of Museums, in terms of approaching the legacy of Jewish history in Germany, are indeed locally negotiated. It is precisely such local processes of negotiation that this study seeks to describe and illustrate.

I have separated this category (political education) from the previous one (memory) as a means to gain a better understanding of the interplay between them. In practice, however, they are very closely linked. James

Young remarks, "Taking a lesson from the Allied efforts at re-education in Germany after the war, museums to the Second World War era in Germany now make memory and pedagogy their twin aims: one comes automatically with the other ... Both aims are accomplished within the context of memorialization" (Young 1988: 183). Harald Welzer characterizes the general endeavor, and more importantly, the expressed goals in Germany as follows:

> The German culture of memory mediating via history classes, political education, memorial-site pedagogy, the media and the wider field of Holocaust Education aims to achieve a historical-moral education, which firstly makes National Socialism and the Holocaust historically accessible, and further aims to form personalities, who would and could oppose mass-murderous or genocidal violence. *Stated educational goals are the training of democratic skills and the development of civil courage.* (This latter emphasis mine; Welzer 2010: 1)[10]

Note the strongly moral component here and the direct connection to "democratic" principles. I would argue too that the term "culture" as in culture of memory (*Erinnerungskultur* in German) should be understood also here as a synonym for discourse. Indeed *Erinnerugskultur* and *Erinnerungsdiskurs* appear very often as synonyms. In my use of the term discourse, I do not simply mean a general idea of a public way of speaking about things, but a much broader use of the term. Kaschuba (2006) describes and develops the issue as follows:

> When we speak of a discourse in its categorical meaning ... then we are referring to at least four qualities. First, the term means a fixed system of argumentation ... secondly, systems of rules are referred to regarding how we are meant to relate to one another in public discourse, which forms of language and argumentations are permissible. Thirdly, discourses describe "systems of thought." ... Finally—what is often and happily forgotten—discourses embody systems of social practice, in which ways of thinking and acting are bound, in which they transmit values in social and cultural patterns of behavior. (Kaschuba 2006: 236–37)[11]

This last point is especially relevant to approaching the material in my study as it is about the museum visit as a social practice meant to reflect certain values. Further, museum visiting is at once a discursive practice and a cultural one. The implications of being inside the prevailing or dominant discourse or transgressing it, though, are important too and become visible in the conflicts/misunderstandings that arise in the museum as a field site and the overall research situation as one particularly charged by expectations of political correctness. I use the term political correctness here to refer to language use and practices that are undertaken in order to avoid offending political sensibilities. I am aware that this term has, at times, been misused (especially by those coming from the political right), as a curbing of freedom of speech. I do not subscribe to this position and see the performance of political correctness (the conscious act of not wanting to potentially give offense) as a choice entered into by those who partake in it. It is a concept that is important in the context of the research session with me and is explored in the chapters that follow.

Articulated Position of the JMB and Visible Tensions

The words of the Director of the JMB, W. Michael Blumenthal, point to the museum's status and one of its goals:

> The Jewish Museum Berlin is no ordinary museum. As a major institution of memory, it occupies a unique place in Germany's capital city. As a national institution supported by the Federal Government, the State of Berlin, all political parties, and a broad cross-section of the public, its mission has socio-political meaning that far transcends the story it tells of the 2,000-year history of German Jewry. It symbolizes, in fact, a widely shared determination to confront the past and to apply its lessons to societal problems of today and tomorrow. (Brodersen, Dammann, and Rossbach 2005: 14)

Here the museum's role as a site of political education is clearly stated. Visitors are meant to "apply lessons" of Germany's tortured history to present-day life. Blumenthal continues by stressing: "We have also aimed to appeal to all visitor interests, with special emphasis on the many young people we hope to attract" (Brodersen et al. 2005: 16). From this, we can infer that the museum hopes especially to teach visiting school groups these lessons.[12]

Another look at part of the interview excerpt mentioned at the end of the previous chapter demonstrates how this connection between memory and political education can start to play out: the speaker, himself a repeated visitor to the museum, coming from an upper–middle class intellectual family, explains:

> what is passed on to us from our parents, from the entire society, is that one has to tackle this topic, that one will still try to prevent any right-wing activities, *that one really very strongly, we as Germans, we who have this history behind us, must fight against this.* When one then sees the victims of that history, as mentioned, the Jews there in this museum, one does get a bit the feeling of guilt and shame because our ancestors were largely guilty of what happened then. (Emphasis mine; TR 3 group interview 13 September 2007: 4)

In this short passage, we see a seemingly natural jump from a form of communicative memory to a sense of political belonging—as Germans—and political action—to prevent right-wing activities related to expressions of sympathy and shame. The fostering of *emotional engagement* as a pedagogical principal is crucial here.[13] In this specific example, the role of political education seems, at first glance, clear-cut. However, a deeper and critical approach is important in order to grapple with the possibilities and implications. What does it mean, "to participate in democratic citizenship?" Who partakes? And who does not? Indeed the notion of a national German memory based on a performance of guilt, shame, or any such affect, when it is linked to having had Nazi ancestors, is highly problematic since it tends to cut off and out those who cannot make this claim. They risk being left outside of the discourse. How does a moral tone interact with emotional engagement? And, most relevant to my study, how does this work in relation to visitor experiences in the JMB? These issues are central. It is not a matter of evaluating the museum's effectiveness in terms of meeting expressed aims, but rather a look at how this context of a morally toned political education relates to doing the museum visit.

It is worth looking at a particular encounter in the museum to highlight some of the tensions between commemorating the Holocaust (with its clear affective dimension), yet proclaiming not to be a Holocaust museum, play out. Here I recall an early interaction with a visitor services staff member, prior to beginning my own work with the school groups.

Customer Service in Red and Black—Can I Help You?

I am looking around the museum to see if there might be a good space for a conversation with a group of future visitors. I look into the Rafael Roth Learning Center, but I see it is roped off.

Then a woman approaches me: "Can I help you?" she asks (in German). She was dressed in black as the visitor services staff are, with a red scarf. This red scarf, quite elegant, actually distinguishes the visitor services staff from other staff. I tell her in German that I would like to bring a school group in the near future and was looking for a good place for a discussion. She replies also in German, which is not always the case, as often when I speak I get replies in English. She says she is happy to help, and if she is not there on the day I come, just find anyone with a scarf like this on. We are here to help you and answer any questions. She was quite forthright and also came across as dominant, but at the same time very, almost aggressively, friendly (like someone in a shop trying to sell me something). Then she suggested that I should actually take the group first to the upper floors where the permanent exhibition starts and then have the kids explore the underground sections at the end of the visit. This is the concept the museum wants to encourage, she says. I am surprised at this, why speed through the section, where you enter? She explains: first, they should learn about the chronology of the history and not begin down here. Otherwise, these sections overshadow the next sections. We don't want this: this is not a Holocaust museum, she stresses. So the visit should start upstairs with the history and end down here with reflection. But the entrance is here, I say. We have to give the tickets in and come down here first. Why was it built this way in the first place? She doesn't address this question directly, but mentions that Libeskind envisioned the stairway up to the permanent exhibition, as a challenge to approach history, and the visitors should do this first at the beginning of the visit. I then ask about how this is actually managed. She replies: well in guided tours, it's easy, the groups are just taken upstairs first. With individuals or smaller unguided groups, it can be tricky. She says she tries to catch people as they first enter the axes, and tell them to go upstairs first: that is to proceed straight across and up the other side. I thanked her for her help and endeavored to watch on other visits how this actually works. I did so, and found the variations in response remarkable (Field diary 16 May 2007).

I am in the museum taking a few photos for my collection and notice the visitor services staff with the red scarf, who had recommended that I first skip the underground sections with my group. I decide to observe her interactions with visitors for a while. Soon enough she approaches an older couple who are walking, looking around a bit after having entered the axes. She speaks to them first in English, asking them if they need directions to the main exhibition. They reply, sure, thanks. I guess they are Americans. She is very polite and tells them to go straight ahead until they see the long stairs up, and that is where the exhibition actually begins. They say thank-you and walk on. But they do not go straight up. They linger in the axes, eventually turning off along the Axis of the Holocaust. Some time later, a school group enters with a guide, speeds through the underground section and straight up the steps. She does not need to approach them, but nods hello to the guide. Later, a group of tourists arrives. They look young, high-school age. They have cameras with them and are speaking Japanese to each other. The visitor services staff member makes a beeline for them and says in loud English, "You must go upstairs first!" They smile at her and nod, but do not move ahead and are still looking around the axes a bit and conversing with each other. Then she goes up to them again. This time she actually puts her hands on the shoulders of one of the young women and faces her in the correct direction toward the Axis of Continuity. She says loudly and forcibly, "The start is up there!," pointing ahead. The young visitor looks intimidated and starts to blush. She replies, "Yes I know, thank you." To which the visitor services staff replies in seeming exasperation: "Yes, but you don't do it. You should go up first!" At this point, I am quite amazed at how much liberty she took with this visitor and wondered what memory of the visit this visitor might take home with her. Maybe that of the aggressive staff member that compelled her to conduct her visit just so? (Field diary 12 July 2007).

Another day another mood. The same staff member in black with her red scarf is at her post near the bottom of the stairs at the entrance. A small group, looks like a family, is coming down the stairs. They are talking in Hebrew to each other. She waits, hesitates for some time, then very politely and quietly in English, says, "There is more upstairs in case you are new to the museum." The man (father?) smiles and says "thank-you," and the group continues along their way. She replies, "You're welcome" and does not approach them again. The family spends quite some time in the underground sections, visiting the Garden of Exile and the Holocaust Tower, before proceeding upstairs (Field diary 19 February 2008).

My reading of these episodes, which did seem bizarre to me at the time, is that they illustrate an uncomfortable consciousness of the fundamental paradox between conflicting, potentially irreconcilable, attested goals of the museum written into the very makeup of the building: that of marking the Holocaust and wanting happy visitors at the same time.

An awareness of pre-existing feelings of local visitors on the topic also helps to put these practices into perspective. This not only came up in my study, but was also an important factor in a front-end (before its opening) evaluation of the JMB, carried out between 1998 and 2000 by Volker Kirchberg. He found that 40 percent of the respondents in his survey noted pre-existing feelings on the topic "ranging from depression and uneasiness … sadness and powerlessness, the self-imposed duty to be emotionally moved all the way to distinctly formulated shock and fury" (Kirchberg 2004: 2). He also recalled that the Project Director, Ken Gorbey, insisted that these "findings be taken into account in all the further planning steps" (Kirchberg 2004: 3 n5). Clearly then, museum staff and planners were and are aware of many of the issues that certain visitors might bring into the museum. This may be part of the reason that they so often stress that the JMB is not a Holocaust museum. It also likely informed the exhibition planning. Further, Gorbey's reaction is indicative of recent shifts in visitor studies to address not only the "what" and "why" of museums, but also the "for whom" (Davidson 2015: 504). The "for whom" is, in this case, an assumed public, where pre-existing negative feelings on the topic are the norm. Kirchberg goes on to describe expectations of potential visitors that the JMB would be a Holocaust museum as "false" (Davidson 2015: 24). He does not question this official position as it appears on the mission statement. Christian Gudehus, in his review of the museum, briefly mentions the museum's stated position, but then quickly dismisses it as "irrelevant" (2002: 3).

I would argue that the expectation that the JMB be a Holocaust museum is neither correct nor false, and that the statement that it is not one is neither relevant nor irrelevant. These binaries are not particularly helpful. The point is one of perspective. It can hardly be read as "false" to position or even experience a museum inside the *Libeskind-Bau* with its evocative (and very memorable) architecture and its Axis of the Holocaust and Holocaust Tower, as a Holocaust museum. The claim, then, that the JMB is "not a Holocaust museum" may well be beside the point from one, very valid perspective, namely of those visitors who read it as one. It is hardly "irrelevant," though, from the perspective of staff—like the visitor services representative and the guides who rush their groups out of the underground sections—who attempt (successfully or not) in their practices to make this statement "true." Consider, too the available tours at the museum: only one of many touch on persecution under National Socialism.[14]

Nevertheless, I do get the impression, especially from scenes like the ones I detailed above, that the museum is fighting with itself (cheerful exhibition versus somber memorial) and perhaps trying to do too much.[15] In thinking about these tensions, comments by the Director of the Jewish Museum in Munich, Bernhard Purin (2008) are worth considering. Alluding to a number of conflicts, controversies, and misunderstandings over the years, he surmises:

> Jewish museums in Germany, even the smallest ones, are expected to do the following: teach young people and adults Jewish history, be it local or broader; explain three thousand years of Jewish culture and religion in a concise manner; and document and remember the Holocaust. And they are expected to do so not only as educational institutions, but also as sites of remembrance both for the victims and for the descendants of the perpetrators. These museums are expected to express the will of German society to fight racism, and to serve as political statements of responsibility. Faced with all these expectations, they are bound to fail. (Purin 2008: 146)

This is indeed quite a daunting list. I would temper Purin's pessimism with another question: does "failure" to meet one of these expectations mean complete failure? If so, they are too high, unattainable even. A museum cannot be all things to all people (even if the JMB tries to come close with everything it has to offer).

Further, I question how genuine and/or realistic some of these goals are. I referred earlier to the JMB's label as "not a Holocaust museum." One might even use the term "brand" to describe such statements. I would posit that, while I do agree that unrealistic demands are put on Jewish museums by their supporters (which tends to be the state), many of these expectations are, in my view, much more akin to advertising claims. Important is that the brand promises to do something. Whether the product is, in fact, new and improved or indeed works consistently as "not a Holocaust museum," for example, is less important than the public relations message the branding sends. The candid conversations with staff also suggest that there is awareness that this particular advertising claim stretches the "truth," as advertisements often do. Perhaps with some of these expectations, it is more about public relations than actual measurable outputs. Indeed, having some experience in museum evaluations and now a lot of experience in visitor studies, I am not sure how I might reliably measure "success" in some of the rather intangible expectations Purin lists.

The Museum as a Source of Pride

Returning now to some of the ways the JMB was positioned by visitors in my study. One of the questions I asked was, "What does it mean to you personally that this museum is in Berlin?"[16] There are some noteworthy patterns visible in the replies to it. A significant number of replies, notably those given by many of the respondents of West German background, and some of those of upper-middle class East German background—all of which attested a personal connection to this history—characterized the museum as a source of pride. The following are some of the typical comments: "I think that having this museum in Berlin means that the whole of Germany is taking responsibility with regards to our Jewish friends" (Questionnaire, hereafter referred to as QR, 28). "Since it is in the capital of Germany, it is an important symbol to show that we have not forgotten the past" (QR 12). And "It's good that this museum is in Berlin as it shows that Germany is dealing with its history. And, in the end, Berlin represents Germany" (QR 85). Many simply attested "pride" at having this museum in "their city" (QR 29). Another mentioned, "that one sees, through the museum, that the country is dealing with its history (which is rather unpleasant for Germany in its content) … I find that it puts Germany in a positive light" (QR 99). Another stated that the museum was a "strong symbol for reconciliation with the Jews" (QR 37). In these replies, aspects of making Germany look good, *Wiedergutmachung,* and atonement come together. John Borneman also came across analogous instances. He relates how Ulrich Raulff, the then editor of the *Frankfurter Allgemeine Zeitung,* put a positive face on facing the Nazi past:

> Raulff concludes optimistically; he observes that no other republic has allowed such a "relentless boring in the ashes (the history of the Third Reich)." It is precisely this that has leant the Federal Republic "an inner freedom from this past." (Raulff 1999; cited in Borneman 2002: 188)[17]

From this perspective then, the museum is not only read as a haunting symbol of a dark past, but also, and perhaps even more importantly for understanding its present and future role, it sends a positive message about Germany today and the efforts being made here to address and thus "be free" from this past. Clearly, these messages are not only meant for the young visitors surveyed here, but also for the larger local and international community. Figures suggest that roughly two thirds of visitors to the JMB come from outside Germany.[18]

Many of the young visitors also reflected on this tourist-magnet side of the museum. While some stated that the museum was *only* important as a tourist attraction,[19] most others suggested that this aspect too was fundamentally connected to the Nazi past and reconciliation in the present. A young man summarized his opinion of the museum as follows: "I find it primarily important that the international (especially Israeli) tourists see that this topic is relevant in Germany. As the capital city Berlin is, in this sense, a showpiece, naturally" (QR 42). Here, one role of the museum is to communicate the message that Germany is dealing appropriately with the topic internationally, but to a very specific implied audience: Israelis. Here then the hope of achieving some kind of *Wiedergutmachung* is clearly expressed.

This aim of projecting a positive image of Germany through a preoccupation with its history is, naturally, not limited to museums. Indeed the wider spectrum of German political education in schools also has important public relations implications. For example, the introduction to a book and CD-ROM package entitled *Learning from History: The Nazi Era and the Holocaust in German Education* lists such objectives:

> We hope that this information assists a broad international audience, in Germany as well as in the English-speaking world, but especially in the United States, which is Germany's most important transatlantic partner. The CD-ROM presents young people, who are typical for many Germans. With great energy and commitment, they attempt to understand this probably most difficult chapter of German history.... The editors and sponsors hope that the project ... will also contribute to intercultural understanding. ... It is not well known internationally that this dark chapter in German history has been taught for decades in the classroom, especially in upper division high school history courses. (Brinkmann et al. 2000: iv)

In this case, the most desired audience is in the United States and the text projects "typical Germans." Since this booklet was published in 2000, it has likely indeed become clearer internationally that marking aspects of this history are priorities in political education in Germany. The JMB is one very visible illustration of this emphasis, and this is reflected in the role that these visitors explicitly attributed to it. The fact that the museum is also a very visible stage makes it a place where positive messages about Germany can be deliberately manufactured and projected.

In contemplating the replies by the visitors I have just outlined above, I have found it productive to recall Stuart Hall's concept of encoding and decoding. He describes

> a *dominant-hegemonic position.* When a viewer [in my case a museum visitor] takes the connoted meaning from, say, a television newscast or current affairs programme [or in my case a museum space] full and straight, and decodes the message in terms of the reference code in which it has been encoded, we might say that the viewer is "*operating inside the dominant code.*" (Emphasis in the original; Hall 1980: 136)

It does appear here that the visitors mentioned above were indeed operating inside the dominant code.[20]

That this code is far-reaching and powerful becomes all the more evident when observing how the museum space is actively politicized at the highest levels.

A Gala Event—From Pride to Leadership

On the evening of 27 September 2010, I attended the opening of an exhibition on Slave Labor at the JMB. It was a rather lavish affair with a wine reception. I was with my friend and colleague Irit Dekel, a sociologist who has done extensive fieldwork, not unlike my own, at the Holocaust Memorial in Berlin. As the speeches began, we were both admittedly a little put off by what we perceived as the overtly self-congratulatory ring of the speeches emphasizing what a great accomplishment it was to finally have an exhibition on this topic. But it was Christian Wulff, the then president of the Federal Republic, who in his own concluding remarks summed up one key function, and arguably the main function of this gala evening and perhaps of the exhibition itself:

> Today with this festive exhibition opening, we direct our gaze toward the past and the future. Here in the Glass Courtyard of the Jewish Museum this is epitomized in the meeting of the baroque *Kollegienhaus* and the post-modern building by Daniel Libeskind. History reflected upon can show us where humanity has erred in the past. Only they who know these mistakes can hope and work towards avoiding them in the future and to choose a righteous path. Former slave laborers and

> their families now experience a Germany that takes on its historical responsibility. (Wulff 2010)[21]

So, it is crucial here to show a responsible Germany today. Further, Germany in its memory and exhibition practices is projected as a model for others to follow. In President Wulff's words, this exhibition can "Direct the path toward future ways of remembering" (Wulff 2010).[22]

> Exhibitions like this one then can demonstrate Germany's democratic credentials: And you, Mr. President, deserve thanks, because you do, through your patronage and your presence here today, not only honor the victims, but you also underline the significance of critical, historical self-determination for the development and preservation of humane and democratic culture. (Speech on the same occasion by Prof. Volkhard Knigge; Knigge 2010)[23]

In other words, a good part of the intended—and often enough received—message of this institution, emphasized by events like this exhibition opening, might be summed up as follows: Nazi Germany may have been the worst of the worst, but Germany today is among the best and indeed can lead the way in how to remember. Note, too, the position of the Federal Republic on Turkey's proposed membership in the EU being dependent on its remembering the Armenian genocide appropriately, which has been widely reported in the press. In this scenario, we see how the culture of memory can be wielded as a tool of political power. Irit Dekel has also captured an element of a "new" German patriotism in the context of her own work surrounding the Holocaust Memorial:

> For instance, the chair of the Central Council of Jews in Germany, Ms Charlotte Knobloch reflected on Germans' celebration of their national flag during the 2006 World Cup in an interview in the center-left weekly *Zeit* (Knobloch 2006). She stated that "Germans need new patriotism," one that will incorporate the memory of the Holocaust into German national identity in a way that will leave room for loving one's country. Knobloch recounts Habermas' (1995) critical approach to reflective memory work as a way to create many political understandings. This is an act willingly performed by civilians in a constitutional democracy. (Dekel 2014: 78)

Let us keep in mind too that from certain perspectives these institutions—the JMB and the Holocaust Museum—work together. This came up more than once with the visitors who seemed to read these as a unit, either complementing or doubling. Further, both these highly visible constructions are part of a much wider discourse where memory and national-political belonging (a term I prefer to "identity" again for its verbal hence processual quality) are negotiated and entangled.

Returning for a moment to the "typical Germans" mentioned in the booklet intended to inform those in the United States of the commitment to Holocaust education in Germany: one might want to ask the question here: who is excluded from such presentations and what sort of intercultural understanding is meant? Addressing such questions opens up issues of belonging and the problematic of fixed ideas of "culture." Such openings, in turn, challenge a monolithic rhetoric of national belonging. These questions inform my analysis of those situations in which groups did not behave as "typical Germans" might. These questions are developed in later chapters through a close reading of the museum encounters experienced by those visitors who fell outside of the dominant performance of remembrance.

We return next, however, to those who expressed having been deeply moved—*Betroffenheit*—by the museum and the story it tells.

Notes

1. See, for example, Halbwachs 1941, 1952.
2. I use this term as defined by Hirsch (1992). She writes, "In my reading post memory is distinguished from memory by generational distance and from history by deep personal connection ... Post memory is mediated through an imaginative investment and creation" (22).
3. Durch Erzählen, Zuhören, Nachfragen und Weitererzählen dehnt sich der Radius der eigenen Erinnerungen aus. Kinder und Enkel nehmen einen Teil der Erinnerungen der älteren Familienmitglieder in ihren Erinnerungsschatz auf, in dem sich selbst Erlebtes und Gehörtes überkreuzen.
4. gemeinsame Erinnerung; ein kollektives Gedächtnis der Deutschen.
5. Auch die einschlägigen historischen Museen und Ausstellungen boomen weiterhin, so dass die Aura des vergangenen Dunkeln in der deutschen Geschichte nach wie vor wirksam scheint. ... Wenn Geschichtsbewusstsein wesentlich auf "gemeinsamem Erinnern" basiert, auf Existenz bestimmter moralischer, kultureller Konventionen der gemeinsamen Verantwortung von Geschichte, dann bedarf es in jeder Gesellschaft dazu immer wieder klarer politischer Ermunterungen und Vorgaben. Es muss eine gesellschaftliche Übereinkunft darüber immer wieder neu ausgehandelt werden.
6. Die Versäumnisse der frühen Jahre konnten nicht einfach repariert werden, weil weder die Anlässe noch die Erinnerungen zu einem wirklich kollektiven Anliegen gemacht wurden ... Nur wenn die Zeiten und die Rituale, wenn die Stimmen und die Orte einerseits offiziell legimiert, anderseits vielstimmig und dicht genug sind, fungieren sie auch tatsächlich als "Archive des kollektiven Gedächtnisses" ... Über solch ein "Zeitarchiv" des Erinnerns verfügen wir im Blick auf die deutsche Geschichte im Nationalsozialismus also kaum.

7. This is the short form for the Active Museum of Resistance against Fascism in Berlin, a citizens' activist initiative arguing against what they saw as a German postwar desire to forget. This body was active in the debates over the plans for the Topography of Terror terrain. For further reading, see Till 2005: 63*ff.*

8. This episode is also recalled in Bishop Kendzia 2014.

9. I had been initially shocked at this intervention by the school principal. Now, however, it no longer surprises me. From my experiences over time with school principals, especially, I have observed a near obsession with public perception on behalf of the more elite public schools (high achieving *Gymnasien,* for example) in Berlin. The school system is extremely competitive and selective. Such schools then want to be sure to attract the best students (which tend to be children of middle class parents) and filter out the rest. This is, of course, very troubling as it increases already existing social marginalization. A thorough exploration of the school system itself is also something that requires further exploration, but is beyond the scope of this study. Social inequalities magnified within the school system, however, form an important framework that helps to put my findings into perspective.

10. Die deutsche Erinnerungskultur zielt über die Vermittlungen des Geschichtsunterrichts, der politischen Bildung, der Gedenkstättenpädagogik, der Medien und des weiten pädagogischen Feldes der *Holocaust Education* auf eine historisch-moralische Bildung ab, die zum einen Nationalsozialismus und Holocaust historisch verständlich machen, zum anderen Persönlichkeiten bilden soll, die sich gegenüber massen- oder völkermörderischer Gewalt widerständig verhalten können. Erklärte Erziehungsziele sind das Einüben von Demokratiefähigkeit und die Entwicklung von Zivilcourage.

11. Wenn wir also von einem Diskurs in seiner kategorialen Bedeutung sprechen … dann wird damit Bezug genommen auf mindestens vier Qualitäten. Zum einem meint der Begriff ein festes Argumentationssystem … Zum zweiten sind damit Regelsysteme angesprochen, wie im öffentlichen Diskurs miteinander umzugehen ist … welche Sprach- und Argumentationsweisen dabei zulässig sind. Zum dritten beschreiben Diskurse "Denksysteme" … Viertens schließlich—was gerne vergessen wird—verkörpern Diskurse auch soziale Praxissysteme, indem sie Denkweisen und Handlungsweisen miteinander verbinden, indem sie Werte in soziale und kulturelle Verhaltensmuster übertragen.

12. I have previously published these insights in Bishop Kendzia 2011. Reprinted in part with permission from hep verlag AG © 2011.

13. For a discussion of narrative museums and emotional engagement, see Kirshenblatt-Gimblett 2000: 7. There is also a long history of debate on the appropriateness of affective involvement in teaching about the Holocaust. Some arguing that this topic should be presented as-matter-as-factly as possible, while others arguing the need to engage on an emotional level too. The issue will hardly be resolved here. I myself have touched on this in Bishop Kendzia 2012 and would also recommend Van Alphen 2002 and Hooper-Greenhill 2006 on this much-debated topic.

14. Tour topics change regularly. At the time when I conducted my research, only
    one out of eleven tours listed highlighted the Holocaust. For tours available
    today (most of which also focus on issues not related to the persecution of
    the Jews), see https://www.jmberlin.de/en/tours. Naturally, if one is looking
    for persecution stories, there is a vast amount of rich material and workshops
    (with witnesses of the time and access to the archives, for example) that do
    focus on Holocaust history. Clearly, the Holocaust is not ignored. It is rather
    left out and/or underemphasized for certain audiences. For example, when
    I went with my children on a Hanukkah tour in German, nothing negative
    came up at all: no Nazis, no Holocaust. My daughters listened to the Hanuk-
    kah miracle story and played a dreidl game, which my youngest won: she was
    rewarded with a pack of kosher gummy bears. So, too in this moment, the
    JMB was indeed "not a Holocaust museum."
15. Other interactional specifics in this ethnographic moment are also interesting
    and point to the visitor services staff member reading visitors differently and
    acting accordingly. Here I cannot posit any cause and effect, but I do find
    her reticence to the Israeli visitors and friendly politeness to the Americans
    (later I gather that this couple were from New York) and to myself versus the
    downright rudeness to the young Japanese woman remarkable. I return to
    examples of unequal treatment of visitors in later chapters. For an insightful
    illustration and analysis of another interaction between Israeli visitors and a
    guide at the JMB, see Rogoff 2002.
16. This particular question was inspired first by my own initial impressions that
    this museum's location was inseparable from its status and role.
17. Raulff schließt optimistisch; er beobachtet, dass keine andere Republik je solch
    "unablässiges Bohren in der Asche (der Vergangenheit des Dritten Reiches)
    zugelassen habe" und dass gerade dies der Bundesrepublik "eine innere Frei-
    heit gegenüber der Vergangenheit" verliehen habe (Raulff 1999).
18. These figures are reflected in a number of published sources, for example,
    Feldman and Peleikis 2014: 46.
19. Ten respondents indicated this. None of these indicated a personal connec-
    tion to the history. Further, there were some visitors, who indicated that this
    museum's presence in Berlin was of no significance to them. These findings
    are explored in later chapters.
20. I should add that the encoding/decoding model, which appears static, cannot
    account for all the variations in readings that came up in the ethnographic
    material. I return to this shortly.
21. Heute richten wir mit der feierlichen Eröffnung der Ausstellung den Blick
    auf Vergangenheit und Zukunft. Hier im Glashof des Jüdischen Museums
    wird dies durch das Aufeinandertreffen des barocken Kollegienhauses mit
    dem postmodernen Gebäude von Daniel Libeskind deutlich. Reflektierte
    Geschichte kann uns zeigen, wo die Menschheit in der Vergangenheit Irr-
    wege gegangen ist. Nur wer diese Fehler kennt, kann hoffen und dafür ar-
    beiten, sie in Zukunft zu vermeiden und zum Guten zu wenden. Ehemalige

Zwangsarbeiterinnen und Zwangsarbeiter und ihre Familien erleben jetzt ein Deutschland, das sich seiner historischen Verantwortung stellt.

22. Wege zum zukünftigen Umgang mit Erinnerung aufzeigen.

23. Und Ihnen, Herr Bundespräsident, gebührt Dank, weil Sie durch Ihre Schirmherrschaft und Ihre Anwesenheit heute nicht nur die Opfer ehren, sondern die Bedeutung kritischer historischer Selbstvergewisserung für die Entwicklung und Bewahrung humaner Gesellschaft und demokratischer Kultur unterstreichen.

Chapter 3

BETROFFENHEIT

The Museum Visit as an Embodied Memorial Experience

Between Emotional Engagement and Political Correctness

First, I need to clarify this term: *Betroffenheit*. The direct translation I offered above as a state of "being moved" is inadequate. It does not fully capture how the term is used in its German application vis-à-vis coming to terms with the Nazi past. Here, there is a clear tone of guilt/atonement and implicatedness attached to it, which colors the term significantly. For this reason, I prefer to use the German word rather than an English term (dismay) that often appears in translations of it.

As I grapple with the material, two statements, both from experts in this field for whom I have great respect and admiration, keep pushing their way to the forefront of my mind. I think this is happening since they capture a fundamental conflict that the material I have gathered—and been part of—has thrown into sharp relief. The statements are the following. First, Jürgen Habermas wrote in a letter to Peter Eisenman—the architect of the Memorial to the Murdered Jews of Europe—that this monument "should be a sign that the memory of the Holocaust remains a constitutive feature of the ethico-political self-understanding of the citizens of the Federal Republic" (Young 2000: 199). Let us remember that this monument was conceived by its most vocal initiator, Lea Rosh, in a spirit of *Betroffenheit* as a way for the Germans to say, "We are sorry!"[1] I have come also to ask myself which citizens Habermas had been referring to. Who is in the position to say sorry? And the second: James Young in his earlier work characterized public memorials and similar institutions as being "geared toward creating a shared memory—or at least *the illusion* of it" (My emphasis; Young 1993: 6).

The difficulty that I explore in this next section revolves around the one I experienced in interpreting situations, which oscillate between presentations of genuine feelings and connection to the museum, on the one hand, and frustration with the expectations to present in this way. I have done this because the material I have collected and explored over the years has convinced me that "between" is a key word in the title, in that, it comes closest to capturing the practices of a good many of the visitors in this study—not to mention doing justice to the complexities of the situations. The word "between" eschews simplistic binaries without ignoring important patterns, and this is crucial in examining the material.

A Solemn, Timid Even, Start to the Visit

I am at the museum today with a group of senior history students from an upper-middle class neighborhood in what was once a part of West Berlin. We arrive at the museum; inform the attendant outside that we are there. I ask the group if I should explain the security procedure. No, not necessary, they know it. We go down the steps and gather for a moment together in the underground axes. The class splits up rather quickly into gender-based groups. A group of young women is especially quiet, but they do chat about the wall displays. The movement is slow and reserved. With arms at their sides or crossed across the chest, they look around a little. Up, down, then at me.

They seem to be waiting for me to do something. I say they can go ahead to wherever they like. So we move along the path slowly. We pass the Rafael Roth Learning Center, and part of the group goes in and spends a few minutes there, looking intently and reading some of the displays. They spend about five minutes here. One young man sits at a computer terminal and begins using it. Four members of the group leave then. The young man at the terminal remains. I go with the rest of the group.

There happens to be a tour going on, and many from the group stop to listen as the guide explains that Auschwitz is the way into nothing, this is why this path is black—the Axis of the Holocaust that is. I note the desire for guidance even though they have been here more than once before.

A few then move along, others say they feel lost and are not sure where they should go from here. They tend to go toward the Holocaust Tower. I am now with a group of young women. They pause in front of the door. I see that they want to enter, but do not. The young woman who was attending the door is now making a phone call at the internal phone on the wall beside the door to the tower. She puts her hand up in a stop signal. She does not want anyone to go in the Holocaust Tower. So we wait. The attendant does not say anything to us, just continues her conversation on the phone. I do not catch what she is saying, but she seems annoyed and her displeasure is visible.

The women decide they do not want to go into the tower now. They will try later and double back the way they had come. The annoyed attendant leaves. I stay. I then see four young women from the class approach the tower. They ask me if they can enter. I open the door, and we enter. We spend some time there. No one speaks or utters a sound. They look up and walk around a bit. They are still and silent. Then after quite some time (it felt to me like several minutes), one whimpers: "May we leave now?" Oh dear, I realize they think they have to wait to be "let out." They want permission from me. I say "of course," and we exit together. I ask the young woman who had whimpered why she thought she had to wait to leave. She said that on her previous visits, someone always opened the door for them to enter and then a few minutes later for them to leave.

After this, we make our way to the Axis of Exile. Here I notice the group walking toward us who had previously wanted to enter the Holocaust Tower and say that they can go in now if they want, that we just came from there. Another young woman asks to go outside (to the Garden of Exile), but there is no one there to manage the door. I walk to the door and open it. Oh, she hadn't realized that she could just go out. She also said that she hesitated to just go out as they did not want to get in trouble with the staff and thought they were not allowed to go out since they had been previously prevented from entering the Holocaust Tower. Here I make a mental note how much this trip seems very much a continuation of school for them—complete with rules and asking permission—as one might to ask a teacher if one can leave the class to use the bathroom. I am somehow in the "teacher" role, and they are very well-behaved "pupils." I was also a bit shocked at the grumpy attendant and thought that her offering no explanation for preventing the group from entering the Holocaust Tower earlier and then just leaving was rather unprofessional and certainly not the service I had been used to seeing and getting in my many previous visits to the museum.

Now others from our class come outside to the Garden of Exile. The young men tend to walk deliberately among the columns. Two women secure themselves on the sides of the columns as they proceed. Many go back to read the signage and again proceed to walk among the columns. They then look up and point to the vegetation growing out of the tops of the columns. The atmosphere is somber and the body language still reserved, but the conversation is noticeably louder than the hushed conversations or silence inside. Two of the women come to me and mention what a confusing feeling they get in this garden. One reads the sign on the way to this structure, which specifically asks the visitor to think about "the confusion that exile brings." She certainly seems to be doing this, as she spends quite some time walking among the columns even though it looked uncomfortable for her (Field diary, 11 September 2007).

In analyzing this episode, I find Irving Goffman's insights on "occasioned behavior" (1963: 172) to be useful guiding tools; Goffman recalls, "regulations of conduct are largely traceable to the social occasion in which they occur" (20) and that more specifically "occasioned activity requires involvement in some kind of cognitive and affective engagement" (36). Based then, on the experiences I described, it seems that at this point in the visit, the particular occasion is one which obliges a certain amount of affect (173) on the part of these young visitors. The "bodily idioms" (34), themselves "conventionalized and normative" (35), suggest engagement and involvement with the evocative architecture in the museum. Further, there seems to be a strong desire to do the right thing, not to put a foot wrong, in the repeated asking for permission and my need to tell them more than once that they were indeed free "to do what they liked."

The continuation of school aspect is also important here. It suggests that any separation between work and leisure becomes blurred. Thus, the visit is far more like school "work" than touristic leisure, although aspects of a touristic experience come up even within the memorial activity. Dean MacCannell in his 1976, and now standard, work, *The Tourist: A New Theory of the Leisure Class,* makes clear distinctions between work and leisure, which in the situations outlined here, become unsettled (MacCannell 1976: 34).[2]

For more on how the visitors from this group contextualized their visit, let us turn now to some of the replies, relevant to this excerpt, in their questionnaires. In this case, I explore both the pre- and post-visit questionnaires since all these participants had been to the JMB before. In addition, information about their previous positioning on this topic is essential to understanding their visits. Some general points first. All of the visitors indicated a high level of background information on this topic, the vast majority of it from outside of school time, for example from discussions in the home with family (several times mentioning parents and grandparents, and even giving their parents' professions as historians, teachers, and one sociologist). Further, all but one indicated that their parents had been from West Germany and of German nationality. (The one exception indicated parents from former East Germany.[3]) They had indicated having read books independently, having been on trips to several Holocaust memorial sites in Germany, some even abroad, and having watched more films and television documentaries than could fit on the page. (Several replies to question 1.10, "Where have you already heard, read, or seen something about Jewish history in Germany?," on questionnaires 25–45.) In response to question 1.11, "Which feelings do you personally connect with Jewish history (up to the present) in Germany?," many indicated feelings such as guilt, shame, rage, and horror. The mention of guilt and its appropriateness came up repeatedly and not just with these particular visitors. Some remarkably nuanced conversations formed part of the discussions. These will, naturally, be explored later. But for now I do want to bring up one young woman's questionnaire reply on this question, which I think illustrates concisely the tensions that arose around the topic of German guilt:

> Thinking about what was done to the Jewish people makes me shiver. It is terrifying that people were capable of something like this. But somehow, the history is so far away and yet so near in that it is continually revived (which is also not wrong). But, I do not personally feel guilty for what the Germans did, as I was not even born yet. But, it does always follow one, when one is on holiday and speaks German. (QR 25, Reply [Hereafter refers as R] 1.11)

The mentioning and rejecting of guilt (as opposed to the several replies which clearly stated that they felt it) is tempered by this "but" and being followed/haunted by it, especially when one's Germanness becomes marked, as it can be when one travels abroad. Therefore, guilt is "somehow" in the air even as it is rejected.

In terms of the actual experiences in the underground sections of the museums, typical replies indicated strong negative feelings and an identification with the victims of the Holocaust: one of the young men wrote of his feelings of: "confinement, anxiety" and in the tower "inferiority, uncertainty" (QR 26, R 2.3). One of the young women, who had been with me in the tower mentioned "uneasiness" and "fear" (QR 25, R 2.3). Another wrote, "It was depressing; I imagined that it reflects a bit the feeling of the Jews at that time" (QR 29, R 2.3). While two of her classmates who had also been in the tower with me elaborated in a similar tone:

> All the impressions that one gets in the Garden of Exile, in the Holocaust Tower and in the memory void, are overwhelming time and again. And they are very good to get at least a slight idea of what happened to the Jews between '33 and '45 (QR 31, R 2.2) [and] The mood in the Holocaust Tower is indescribable … I automatically connect this room with the Holocaust. It is depressing as there is only this one sliver of light and one imagines in horror all the terrible things that happened to the Jews. (QR 40, R 2.3)

The behavior in the museum and these replies do suggest that the visit in these sections of the museum was conducted very much as an embodied memorial activity (Connerton 1989). The JMB visit constituted a time and place to contemplate the Holocaust, a topic to which these young visitors had cultivated a personal connection over time. Further, the solemn nature of the occasion is visible in their quiet, respectful behavior as befitting a memorial-like activity. A conscious awareness of this was indicated by an outspoken young man, who will come up again, in a group discussion on the appropriateness of guilt. He wrote simply, "the visit was pleasant since the people here behave more calmly and more consciously than in other museums" (QR 42, R 2.6). Indeed, during his visit many of the visitors were more calm and conscious than, for example, in nonmemorial museums. He too marks the occasion as such, but what he does not mark is "the people." His use of the present tense indicates he is referring to visitors generally, not just to his own group. This generalization then portrays as universal something that is, in fact, particular. I do see that the group he was with behaved in a calm and deliberate manner in doing this visit. This is the norm of his group, and I would argue that this norm should be understood and positioned—or marked—as such, rather than remain unmarked as something universal or common to all "the people" who visit the JMB. The assumption of being in a position to describe others generally, especially of having the legitimacy to explain "how things are in Germany"—naturally purporting to speak for all Germans without marking one's own position, came up on a number of occasions—but only by upper–middle class men of West German background. No one else claimed this right/privilege to explain. Deviations from this norm of conducting the visit as a memorial activity, and their social implications, will be explored in detail in Chapters 4 and 5. Let us return again to this same group at a later point during their visit.

The Memorial Occasion Continues:
The Menashe Kadishman Installation

We are upstairs and the group has been going though parts in the main exhibition with relaxed, but still clearly displayed, interest … A young woman peers down through a window and calls me over. She asks, "What is that down there, and how do we get there?" She is pointing to the installation by the Israeli artist Menashe Kadishman entitled "Shalechet" (Fallen Leaves).

I then lead her and some others from the group to this space. Once down there, I see that many have found it on their own. Fallen Leaves is an immediate hit. It seems to resonate with these visitors. They spend quite some time here and that toward the end of a long visit. Note: it has been well over two hours by now. The mood is respectful. There is almost no talking. They read the sign that invites them to walk over the metal structures—these "fallen leaves."

They all at some point, after some hesitation, do walk over them. The young men deliberately, but with care. One young woman timidly, another more dancingly. She is suddenly shocked by the sound they make under her feet. "Oh, sorry!," she says. Soon, it is time to regroup and go to the meeting point. I think, what a pity, I imagine they would have liked more, and despite my tiredness, I too would have liked to explore the museum further with them, trying to imagine it through their eyes. Their enthusiasm was rubbing off on me (Field diary from 11 September 2007).

In addition to the Holocaust Tower, this installation is something that impressed these visitors the most, as they indicated on their post-visit questionnaires. It was in the group discussion regarding this installation that an illustrative conflict over the role of guilt arose. Let us revisit the conversation briefly mentioned in the first chapter. One of the young women who had walked over the *Fallen Leaves* contextualized the experience as follows:

> What I found pretty cruel was that one did not have the opportunity … I mean, one had the opportunity to demean the people, if I interpret it this way, by walking over the faces, so one had no opportunity at all to do something nice for them or to express one's sympathy. One could only … so I found that a bit guilt inducing … I found it unpleasant to have such guilt imposed that one does not have at all. So, one felt guilty there for something that people once did. It was not as if one looked in from outside what was done by whom to whom, but rather than one was oneself put in such position. There was nothing constructive there. It is in any event interesting to experience this, how it feels to be guilty, but I found it a bit mean actually. (TR 3 group interview 13 September: 3–4)

In this reaction, she suggests that she felt that she was "meanly" compelled into assuming the role of a perpetrator with the corresponding guilt.[4] The metal structures became people whom she could not help, but only demean in the act of walking over them. She complains that it was unproductive, mean, and unpleasant. Young women in a later group, who had a similar reading of this installation, actually refused to walk over it. Two gave the following explanation in the group interview:

> I also wanted to say that it was sort of like a cemetery for me, as if one were to walk over graves, to hop on the graves or the like. So, that is how I saw it, like graves, since at that time the Jews were not individually buried. And it is like a memorial to remember the dead. And so I would not have felt at all well with the idea of walking over them. (TR 6 group interview 9 November 2007: 2)

In addition, her classmate said, "I also did not walk over them, because I remembered a film in which there were thousands of corpses, and soldiers walked over them as if it were nothing. And so I could not do that" (Ibid.). Here, there was different museum activity in that these young women did not walk over the metal structures. These readings are, nevertheless, also ones associated with perpetratorhood complete with media-inspired images of soldiers walking over corpses. What is different here is the visitors' refusal to "reenact" this. My reading of these visiting practices in the Holocaust Tower and with the Kadishman installation is in line with what Ernst van Alphen has called a "traumatic reenactment" or "Holocaust effect" (van Alphen 1997: 81). Van Alphen goes on to specify the crucial role of emotion in such reenactments.

> "Mastery" then, is no longer an epistemic mastery of what happened but a performative mastery of the emotions triggered by the happenings. Only by working through knowledge that is not "out there" to be passively consumed but rather "felt" anew time and time again, by those who must keep in touch with the Holocaust, can art be effectively *touching*. (emphasis in the original; van Alphen 2001: 82)

A powerful affective element is central to participating in this memorial activity, and even the refusal to reenact is a memorial activity. The young women "recall" graves or soldiers and do not "feel comfortable" or "well" with the idea of walking over them.

Back again to the group discussion in the classroom: the outspoken young man, who had so enjoyed the calm and deliberate visit, responded to his classmate's complaint that *Fallen Leaves* was guilt inducing as follows:

> I must say that we did not live through all that and that it [the Nazi time] has been told to us and, in the end, we are not responsible. And yet, what is passed on to us from our parents, from the entire society, is that one has to tackle this topic, that one will still try to prevent any right-wing activities, that one really very strongly, we as Germans, we who have this history behind us, must fight against this. When one then sees the victims of that history, as mentioned, the Jews there in this museum, one does get a bit the feeling of guilt and shame because our ancestors were largely guilty of what happened then. (TR 3 group interview 13 September 2007: 4)

And shortly thereafter, another young man refers directly to her complaints:

> One really has to keep in mind that something horrible happened and that one has to do, really must do, everything within one's power so that such a crime does not occur. I also find this connection between German and Jewish history as portrayed in this museum interesting. That one very clearly sees there that German history and Jewish history are very closely connected, that they are bound together. It is part of our culture of memory to go to the Jewish museum and see these exhibitions and to get these feelings that Luisa has just described, these feelings of sadness, these feelings of pain that one just gets there. This is part of our culture because it is all our history; [it] belongs to our culture. (TR 3 group interview 13 September 2007: 4–5)

Here then, the young men assert that guilt, shame, and even having unpleasant feelings in the museum is a constitutive part of being "German," which is traceable to knowledge that their ancestors had been the perpetrators. Also crucial is the recognition that this has been passed on to them by "their parents and the whole society." In other words, these young men claim a culturally (learned by and in society) and ethnically (it is because our ancestors were the perpetrators) based ownership of the topic. I, at times, refer to this narrative "great-granddad was a Nazi after all" as indicative of a contrast to the widely read and often cited research of Harald Welzer with members of the previous generation of "very ordinary Germans." The book was entitled: *Grandpa Was No Nazi (Opa war kein Nazi)*. Welzer describes how in the subsequent generations there emerged the need to construct a past in which their own relatives had nothing to do with the crimes (Welzer, Moller, and Tschuggnall 2002).

In the group discussion, the young men went on to further characterize guilt as a normal part of being German in contrast to other nationalities:

> A year and a half ago I was there [at the JMB] with a French friend, so someone who is not Jewish, not German … But for him these feelings, described by Luisa, of guilt were not evoked, but rather (I spoke with him in French now) I would say it was awe and respect for the suffered history that was evoked, if the "personal connection" is missing. If he was not a Frenchman who somehow had Vichy or such collaborators as parents, so more of an outsider. So, he was very impressed with the museum and said that it was very much respect inducing when one sees it in person. (TR 3 group interview 13 September 2007: 8)

And his classmate replies immediately:

> I also believe that we, so specifically the Germans, feel the most guilty there. We may not have lived through it, but still the whole history always comes to this point. At least this is how I see it. I can deal with it. It is nothing bad, but it does make me ever alert so that something like this does not happen again. I believe that these feelings are strongest among the Germans, both among the youth and also among adults. In contrast to some Jewish fellow citizens who go there or those from abroad. I believe that in those cases there is more respect, but that the emotions are not so strong when they go there. Except maybe among the Jewish fellow citizens, but the other tourists not so strong. (Ibid.)

I admit that I was at once impressed and surprised at such strong and sophistically worded ownership by these eighteen-year-olds of this *Erinnerungskultur* centered on guilt. Impressed by the conviction and eloquence, and surprised, as I perceived a stark contrast between the messages I got and get from my friends and neighbors in Berlin (those who know me as "Victoria" and not as the "Canadian Researcher"). Conversing informally over coffee, or on my children's playground, the predominant message I had received about this topic (on the few occasions that it came up) was and is, "It is too much already! We have had enough!" Only twice on the questionnaires from this group did similar complaints come up. As one young man wrote of the JMB: "It was very Holocaust-laden, what is also clear … one had the feeling in the entire underground section of being guilty and so of having to feel bad" (QR 27, R 2.1, 2.3). This young man seemed to have remained silent in the group interview. Another young man expressed similar sentiments—again only on the questionnaire—as follows:

> the feeling that the German-Jewish past generates the compulsion to have to dedicate oneself exclusively, especially in the years just preceding high school, to literature and books for young people about the Jewish problematic. As a result, other educational materials are withheld from the pupils, for example in German class. (QR 32, R 1.11)

Interestingly, such Holocaust fatigue, a phenomenon that is widely perceived, does not however prevent these young visitors from claiming Holocaust memory as theirs and approaching the museum accordingly. Their body language in the museum was solemn and sober, and this was followed by expressions of guilt and of being made to feel guilty.

Let us recall the idea of remembrance once again as something that is performed, but that does not necessarily correspond to internal states. This concept is key to exploring the visiting behavior of another group of highly engaged participants—not unlike this group in terms of doing the visit—but with a noteworthy variation.

Betroffenheit without Guilt?

I am waiting in the teacher's room in a Gymnasium in a solid upper–middle class part of what was once East Berlin … Ms W. enters, and we are introduced to her. She makes an immediate good impression on me. Young, significantly younger than myself, I would judge, is very relaxed in jeans and a loose sweater. She dresses a lot like many of the students at my institute. I imagine I would get along with her and have a laugh over a drink if the circumstances were different. She is very supportive of the project and chatty.

Her manner with her students is just as relaxed. She sits on the desk as she speaks to them. She hardly raises her voice. She also does not need to. The students make a very mature impression. I am a bit surprised that this is a grade eleven class. They easily seem older and quite composed.

I explain my project, and they display interest. All indicate they would like to take part, with nods, still reserved though. One young man seems particularly enthusiastic. It is also a large group (ca. thirty). Like with the group in the former West Berlin upper–middle class area, I do not see any visible minorities. Many indicate that they have been to the JMB before and do go to museums regularly in their free time.

I also field the occasional question as they are filling in the pre-visit questionnaires. One young woman asks, "What if I don't know if the town my parents came from was in the East or West?" I say just to write the town and "Bundesland" (state, province) down, and I can check it later.

They fill out the questionnaires in about twenty minutes. Quite a bit of writing. I thank them again and confirm the time and meeting place for tomorrow's visit. I offer to give directions to the JMB, but they all seem to know where it is already!

It is now late afternoon, and I am home. This school is quite some distance from my home, really at the other end of the city. I am tired, and I briefly review the questionnaires they had filled in. A few things stand out. From this class, far fewer (only three women and one man, out of twenty-seven) made any mention of "guilt" or "shame" as feelings they associate with the topic. Further, they all indicated a high degree of background knowledge, including conversations with family, trips to a number of Holocaust memorial sites in Germany and abroad (including Israel for three respondents), a great deal of reading, and film/TV viewing—in short in this respect, these replies were very similar to the comparable group in the former West. But they differed on the "guilt" issue and in one other respect. In the earlier group, the majority of the replies (fifteen out of twenty-one) indicated they were Christian. In this group, only five indicated being Christian. The rest (twenty-two) wrote that they were Atheists or had "no religion." My first impression had been that there were no Germans of non-German background; this was confirmed by their replies. They were German-born to parents who had been East Germans. Two indicated one non-German parent, but they defined themselves as German. I am now tired having gone over the numbers, but am looking forward to the day tomorrow (Field diary from 6 November 2007).

I am standing outside the main entrance a few minutes before ten o'clock. Two students approach me. One is a young man, and I ask him if he knows the security procedures. Yes, he says, I have been here several times. "How many?" I ask. "Five," he replies. I ask him for what, "Once with the school for a particular exhibition about numbers, another time with his father, then with some tourist friends." I think to myself, wow after five visits, he still wants to visit again. He also mentions that he comes regularly for various temporary exhibitions. He says there is a lot to see, so he is here for this trip too. More of the students gather, and they also know the drill and do not have to be told to go through security one at a time. They are surprisingly quiet for such a big group. After getting the tickets, the visit begins. Most seem to know their way around.

They seem interested, reserved, and respectful here in the axes. There is very little speaking if any. The body language is also reserved, arms often crossed across the chest. The behavior generally could be described as "gepflegt" (cultured) … We make our way along the Axis of the Holocaust, and there is a guide, a young man. He explains, "Here, we have time to contemplate." When the attendant standing beside the Holocaust Tower opens the door, I enter the tower with some of the young men from the class. They are silent and still. They look up. Then some women from our group enter the tower. They seem eager to leave the tower, fidgety and shivering. They seem nervously uncomfortable.

The body language is still reserved here with arms at side and then warming themselves (it is cold!). They do leave the tower after a few minutes. After a moment they speak, but very quietly. They seem unpleasantly moved. I recall that on the way in, one of the women would only go in if her classmate joined her. Due to the wet and cold weather, no one goes out to the Garden of Exile (Field diary 7 November 2007).

These young women and men conducted this part of their visit much like many of the visitors from the previous group. The questionnaire replies regarding this section of the museum were also comparable, with indications of "sadness, fear, depression" (QR 96, R 2.3) and "constriction, fear, sympathy" (QR 95, R 2.3), and a lot of direct identification with the plight of the Jews (QR 76, 78, 79, 81, 84), just to note a few examples.

It was an interaction that began in the museum and carried over into a conflict in the classroom that distinguished this research situation.

Anger at Other Visitors—"They Are Totally Disrespectful!"

About ten members of the group are in the Children's World. One young man draws a picture on the blackboard. Many are sitting and do look tired and possibly bored. The very interested boy from the day before approaches saying he is really disgusted with some of the visitors he had seen just running across the Kadishman installation, exclaiming: "They are totally disrespectful!" He asks if I have been to Yad Vashem. "No," I say. He mentions that he was in Yad Vashem, and that there is a similar installation work there. He then says that I should know that actually most of his classmates are not interested in the topic or the museum, "they just like the fact that they get the day off from school!" I realize at this point that his pre-visit questionnaire was the one that I found so extreme, when I read it the evening before.

I find this sort of confiding in me interesting on many levels. He sets himself apart from the mass of disinterested students. He has been to Israel. He mentions this more than once. He is also a part of a political group for which this topic is very important. He knows the museum well and has been several times. He just finds that most of the German visitors do not take the topic or the museum seriously and do not behave properly. He seems to want to make sure that "the wool is not pulled over my eyes." I should not mistake his classmates' willingness to take part in this study as genuine interest.

I wonder if I give the impression of being particularly gullible or clueless. Or if it is just that I am clearly not German—so do not know the culture as they do—that encourages these sorts of interactions. I am reminded of the group before and the young men there explaining to me "how things are done in Germany" (Field diary 7 November 2007).

That evening I revisited his replies: he had given himself the pseudonym "Amos" (a common Israeli first name), and since I will handle his material at some length, I will refer to him by this name. Amos indicated he was Protestant, but left the item asking for "nationality" blank. Both his parents had been from East Germany. His feelings about this topic, he indicated as follows: "*Betroffenheit,* aggression, anger at present-day society, anti-German attitude, wish for Israeli citizenship" (QR 90, R 1.11). I think it was this rage at present-day German society, followed by his "wish for Israeli citizenship" that most threw me. This vehemently expressed anger at his fellow Germans carried over into his replies about the museum visit throughout the post-visit questionnaire. Rather than indicating his perception of the museum's architecture or exhibition, he repeatedly recalled his annoyance with the other visitors generally and his classmates specifically:

My expectations regarding the ignorance of the group were completely fulfilled. I did not have any great expectations regarding the museum since I have been here often (R 2.1). I did not expect to see so many intolerant, ignorant visitors. Mostly school classes (R 2.2). Annoyed (with ignorant visitors). [This the predominant impression in the Holocaust Tower] (R 2.3). Annoyed, nausea-queasiness with regards to Germany today and German history (R 2.4). [This the prominent impression in the main exhibition] I find it very good. But I have the feeling that the youth do not use it or do not want to concern themselves at all with Jewry, the history, the diaspora (R 2.5). [On the importance of this museum's presence in Berlin; Had his impressions of Jewish history changed after the visit?]. No, they have only diminished my view of present-day society in Germany. I think a lot of people deal with the topic in a wrong way. Besides I see a lot of historical ignorance and a general movement toward the right in this society. … The visit has strengthened my political mind-set. (R 2.7, 2.8)

In fact, he only deviated from voicing his anger twice on the entire post-visit questionnaire. Once to indicate that what he thought he would most remember was: "the Holocaust Tower, the steel faces on the ground, the Garden of Exile" (R 2.10). And, in reply to the question which asks how he enjoyed his visit generally: "Very well, I could recognize similar architecture or exhibits or draw comparisons with the Diaspora Museum, Tel Aviv, with Yad-Vashem, Jerusalem" (R 2.6). In this last reply, he stresses his Israel connection again.

I was, for some time, at a loss about how best to deal with this particular material. It appeared so extreme that to highlight it as somehow representing a visitor-type seemed inappropriate, and the road of least resistance—to skip over it—would have also been problematic. I struggled with how to adequately analyze this without falling into the tempting trap of trying to psychoanalyze Amos—a trap that, I think, would misrepresent the nature of this ethnographic work. It is not so much about the "why" of the social practices, be they partake in an embodied memorial activity, or in a tirade against fellow visitors, but much more about the "how."[5] With this in mind, let us now go to the group interview and see how a rather heated and illustrative conflict arose when I asked the group to elaborate on feelings regarding this history and the museum and mentioned sadness, sympathy, and guilt.

One young man begins:

> I actually think that shame and feelings of guilt are out of place, since it was two generations ago. Of course it is very bad what happened back then. But in the end, it is not as if I had anything to do with it. From this point of view one can also hold the Americans accountable for the large numbers of murdered Indians, or in Russia the opponents of Communism, many millions were murdered there. That's why I don't know if one, now, really has to say "Yes, I'm guilty of it." (TR 6 group interview 9 November 2007: 3)

His classmate (a young woman) continues, "Well, I would also say that I do not have any guilt feelings, since I know that I had nothing to do with it and would also not have … being the kind of person I am. So, I do not identify now with what happened back then in Germany" (Ibid).

Amos speaks up:

> I see it this way, I have sometimes felt somehow guilty when I talk with some Jewish people and they tell me what happened to their families during the war. And I know what my family did during the war. And then I do get feelings of guilt and also a feeling of responsibility for what we did during the war—in that "I am a descendent of the perpetrators." I often feel a sort of respect for Jewish young people.

> I have also discussed this with them. It is not easy for them to separate it, to sit at a table with children of perpetrators as children of victims and to meet.
>
> Now Amos looks directly at the young man who first spoke and in a harsh tone adds: "One should first of all come to terms with things oneself and not refer to others—to look at what happened with oneself!" At this point many join in against Amos and even speak a bit over one another, so that keeping track is difficult: a young woman retorts, "Yes, but we were not even there!" Others concur with nods of heads, and other gestural sings of agreement. Amos struggles to reply. Then a young woman asks him directly, "Why then should we have feelings of guilt?"
>
> Now the class seems exasperated with Amos and many roll their eyes, and shake their heads. Then another young man asks, "Why should one get worked up now about this?" In the end, one can only take care that it does not happen again. But to feel guilty for what happened long before one was even alive? If one lets it happen again, then one could feel guilty. But not because one's own grandparents or whoever had been involved in it. (TR 6 group interview 9 November 2007: 3–4)

In this group discussion, the issue of guilt was rejected by all the speakers except Amos, who claimed his status and guilt as a "descendent of the perpetrators." Interestingly, given his scorn (expressed "for my eyes only" on the questionnaires and during the museum visit), he was remarkably reticent in the classroom with his "I have sometimes felt somehow guilty." His tone, however, became much harsher when he looked directly at and challenged his classmate who had brought up "the Americans" and "the opponents of Communism."

It was not only guilt that was rejected and/or ignored by many of Amos's classmates, but also historical identification at all. Remember, some had not recalled whether their parents had been from the former East or West. This remarkable contrast to the previous group is epitomized in the young woman's statement cited above: "I do not identify now with what happened back then in Germany." I must admit that replies like this one were much more what I had been expecting before I had embarked on this study. Given that outside of the JMB or other such sites, in my daily life, this topic rarely ever came up with people of my own generation or younger.

While I certainly cannot posit a cause and effect that might explain these contrasts, I do think the correlations are interesting: that those who did not attest guilt and later countered Amos's position, for example, all indicated that they were Atheists on the questionnaires. Indeed, only Amos and two others from this group wrote of guilt on the questionnaires. Might there be a connection (more than just a correlation) between Christian religiosity with its associated habitus—as in a "community of learned embodied dispositions" (Bourdieu 1972: 99) with a long tradition of atoning for Original Sin, and the performance of guilt in the context of the Nazi past? This is, naturally, a subject too big to be tackled here. The material I have collected can only posit the question; it cannot supply an answer.

What the material does demonstrate, however, is that there was an attested personal connection to this history in both groups explored so far—that they discussed this topic in the home, for example. What the replies do not show is the *how* of it: whether there was a tone of guilt/atonement in the family discussions. This would have required different methodological tools and is indeed beyond the scope of this study. I can only speculate, and infer from the material, that there might have been more a discourse of guilt practiced in the case of those who attested Christianity and West German background, than by those who attested no religion and East German background. I also have to admit that in terms of observing the doing of the visit, I could hardly have surmised that one type of displayed *Betroffenheit* included guilt and another did not. This possibility only became visible in the questionnaire replies, interviews, and resulting conflicts over whether or not guilt by descent is constitutive of Germanness.

In any event, what emerges here is that common visiting practice, doing the visit as a memorial activity, which outwardly appears to be in harmony with those of other visitors (for example the two groups behaved in very similar ways throughout the visit) does not necessarily mean that the memory is in fact common. I recall here Winter and Sivan's (1999) contributions on "remembrance." This concept is particularly appropriate to these episodes. Both the visiting groups described above could well have belonged to the same informal choir and been performing a sing-along in relative harmony (Winter and Sivan 1999: 28). Sharon Macdonald's (2012) concept "past presencing" is also particularly useful for anthropological work and applies here. Macdonald suggests:

> Past presencing … is intended to draw attention to the multiple ways in which the past may be (and be made to be) present—as well as represented—whether articulated verbally or experienced and performed in other ways." (Macdonald 2012: 3)

Looking again at the conflict with Amos, one sees this dynamic at work: in this exchange, we see Amos moving in and out of a sort of past presencing. First claiming the "we" of the perpetrators, as if he had been there. He then takes on the "descendant of the perpetrators" status, and then again collapses time in challenging his classmate, who had himself brought up the American and Soviet pasts, as arguments supporting his own rejection of guilt, asserting the need to "look at what has happened with oneself." Collapsing time is a strategy inherent to past presencing (Macdonald 2012: 7,

2013: 44). This strategy serves to make the past serve the needs of a given present situation. With the mention of an American and Russian past, the young man aims to counter Amos's assertion. Further, Amos's ownership of this past and his situating it in the present, is in my view, hardly a violation of Germanness per se, but rather a particular display of one type of Germanness in favor of another. He rejects the type that he associates with the Nazi past and then immediately connects with present-day Germans who do not remember appropriately. He claims a version of Germanness that owns Nazi antecedents, expresses guilt, and remains politically active in the present. Recall too that, despite Amos's rather extreme wording and positioning, he is operating clearly within a dominant code of behavior. What is crucial in approaching this episode with Amos and his classmates is that both the concept of remembrance and of past presencing do not insist on actually shared images assumed to be in the minds of the performers. What is shared, however, is the sort of visiting activity itself.

Considering "Performance"

With these situations, I find it fruitful to revisit and elaborate on "performance" as an analytical tool adapted to cope with this material. Richard Sandell in his study on museum audiences: *Museums, Prejudice, and the Reframing of Difference* outlines the issue clearly, and his insights are particularly relevant to my study. Sandell draws on previous work by Le Couteur and Augoustinos on prejudice research, who explain:

> individuals will make different evaluations at different times and in different contexts. Instead of "attitudes," they prefer the notion of "interpretive repertoires" defined as "sets of metaphors, arguments, and terms that are used recurrently in people's discourse to describe actions and events" [Le Couteur and Augoustinos 2001: 218]. In more traditional approaches to prejudice research, researchers have tended to look for consistency in people's "attitudes" and accounts, viewing language as an indicator of relatively stable internal mental representations [Ibid.]. In contrast, an important characteristic in much of discursive research is the variability of the discourse. "What people say depends on the particular context in which they are speaking and the function(s) that the talk may serve. In the ebb and flow of everyday life, the context within which talk occurs and its accompanying function continually shift and change [2001: 217]. Text and talk is therefore *functional, purposeful, constitutive*—it is directed to accomplish certain social tasks. (Emphasis in the original; Sandell 2007: 34–35)

This point, that text and talk is meant to accomplish specific social tasks, is all the more crucial since my study concerns a potentially morally laden context. Further, much of the material is about expressing emotions, verbally and gesturally. The ubiquitous expressions of guilt, sorrow, and shame, for example, and the reserved body language in the museum, in my view do not necessarily point to any stable internal states, but are rather important in terms of performing the museum visit and in many cases even portraying and constituting a certain type of Germanness. These expressions help the visitors to position themselves in relation to the topic—and in relation to others. Understanding this context too is crucial to interpreting the role and function of this museum.

Sharon Macdonald also offers a productive framework that avoids the problematic either/or trap that one can fall into. She notes:

> performance may be—and often is—understood in practice as an enactment of "prior conceptual entities." This does not contradict the point that we should avoid a theoretical framework that assumes that it is always so, but equally, I argue, we need theorising that is able to recognise, and provide an analytical handle upon, the fact that it may be so. If our analytical perspective does not allow us to think of performance in this way, then we can neither tackle cases of calculated or instrumental attempts to use performance to particular ends, nor can we consider questions of fit or discrepancy between the conceptual and the performed. … Recognizing the indeterminacy of performance as a central rather than incidental feature gets us away from the dilemma of seeing performance *either* as a playing out of the previously conceived *or* as only "in itself." Recognizing the indeterminacy of performance means that we can look at it as a process in which meanings are constructed while understanding that it may, to varying extents, entail attempts to act out some idea, to communicate something to an audience. (Macdonald 2006: 11)

Navigating the difficult material in all its messiness is, naturally, central to a nuanced situational analysis. Keeping the indeterminacy of performance in mind helps in the endeavor to avoid stifling binaries (as in it is either true or not, honest or not). This is in turn crucial to evaluating the material presented here and doing justice to the many shades of grey without ignoring the black and white.[6]

Exploring My Role Further—Political Correctness Thrown into Sharp Relief

With all performances, there are audiences either real or implied. In the case of this particular research situation, I, the ethnologist who called this project into being, am an important audience. Here, then, it is especially important to recall Rolf Lindner's (1981) call to take how we as researchers are perceived by the participants seriously and reflect on how that affects the material. There are a number of indicators in the material itself that at first glance may seem minor, but upon more thought, however, do need to be highlighted. One appears in a side scribble in my field diary from a museum visit, where I note—and only later fully recalled—the following interaction with one of the young men: I had mentioned that I had reviewed the pre-visit questionnaires and was impressed with how much they all had read and seen on this topic. He smiled warmly and even put his hand on my back and said something along the lines of, "In Germany it is like this. We have to deal with this topic a lot." My notes only contained the gist of his words, not the exact lines and not even in German—although I know he spoke to me in German (Field diary 11 September 2007). What I think emerges from this episode is my foreignness in his eyes, the assumption that I do not know how things are in Germany. I found this young man's confidence that he is in a good position to tell me how it is not just for him, but moreover, generally "in Germany" striking. The "clueless, nice, Canadian woman" being enlightened by the obliging, polite, male insider. He who takes on a role of speaking for all Germans and Germany.

Next, a question arose at the very end of the group interview, when I thanked this supportive group for their time and asked if they had any questions. Again, one of the most active young men asked: "We were talking among ourselves about you doing this study and what connection you have to it, if you yourself were Jewish" (TR 3 group interview 13 September 2007: 9). When I replied, that while "I myself was not raised Jewish, but my mother had been. So, there is this connection." There were smiles and nods of recognition, which I interpreted as "We thought as much." Then the young man wanted to know what I thought of them. Here the transcript ends, but I remember replying, "I was impressed with the background knowledge, but a little shocked at how oppressive this history still is." This episode makes two points very clear. First, and most importantly I think, is that it makes visible that many in this group perceived me as someone who was potentially "Jewish." They had discussed this possibility among themselves. This is decisive, since it means that the performances were likely not only in order to display a form to German-ness generally, but more specifically, to do so in front of a potentially Jewish audience. This is not to say they were dishonest, but rather that certain aspects were brought up, while others were not. Perhaps this helps to make sense of the very high attestations of guilt versus the very low admissions of Holocaust fatigue that came up, especially in the earlier situations with this group. The realization that this group viewed me as potentially having Jewish background adds new significance to this note on the questionnaire by one of the young women, who claimed a "careful dealing with Jewish topic/behavior towards Jews because of German history" (QR 39, R 11.1). Naturally, these "perhapses" have to remain speculation, as there are limits to how much one can "know" about intentions of the participants, either conscious or not. They do, nevertheless, seem plausible.

This perception of having to be careful on this topic, however, is hardly limited to my study and to direct interactions with Jews (real or potential). It hits at the heart of political correctness and its problems. In a 2010 study conducted by *Zeit Online,* 41 percent of high school students surveyed complained, "One cannot express one's opinion of the Nazi past in Germany honestly" (Stass 2010: 2). While, as I said, I do not believe these participants were being dishonest with me, I do think the silence speaks volumes: the choice not to mention Holocaust fatigue, or boredom in the museum, for example, may well have been conscious and carefully considered ones.

In terms of Amos's presentation of self, while clearly he did not invent his interest in Israel or his anger at Germany for my benefit, he chose to voice them so strongly with me personally (via the questionnaires and the conversation in the museum) since this was a message he wanted me to receive. It becomes, in fact, at this level of argument irrelevant if the emotions mentioned were actually felt (Cf. Crapanzano 1992: 237). I cannot know this, anyway. What is crucial is that these discursive repertoires perform functions of self-construction and self-positioning. Interesting here is that in some cases attesting guilt is a part of this and in other, seemingly very similar cases, it is not. These situations illustrate what can be made visible when one endeavors "to probe behind facades of national unanimity" (Herzfeld 2005: 1).

This constellation—participants, museum, myself as researcher—exemplify, then, the construction Wolfgang Kaschuba describes as "being-so/wanting-to-appear-so" (Kaschuba 2006: 132).[7] This I see as a combination not as a binary "either-or" but rather as a "both-and" issue. It is in this sense that I use the words "in between" in so many of my titles. The material gathered in the field does not lend itself to clear-cut binaries—one can be both emotionally engaged and feel the need to be careful and engaged in "politically correct" practices, for example. Indeed, the presentation of self is a dynamic process and adapts according to the situation as is clear in the later interactions with some of these same participants. One young man mentioning the issue of guilt and responsibility again later added:

> One should also realize that one boasts about all the positive things that have happened in the past that the Germans did. What Germany produced. One still refers to them. One is proud of them—one can name various examples. Yes, Karl Benz invented the automobile, and we are the best automobile makers in the world and

> always have been. … One has to recall the positive things along with the negative things. And that's just part of it. And then one cannot say, "We were born later and have nothing more to do with it." "The grace of having been born too late" is an argument that I do not follow. (TR 3 group interview 13 September 2007: 6)

Here, he shows a time (not during the first meeting) and place (not at the JMB with me) for pride in his country's accomplishments. Further, he has already established his credentials as a thoughtful rememberer and now in minute sixty-five of the interview puts the issue into perspective. Further, he taps directly into the public political rhetoric in the final line where he draws on, and distances himself from, former Chancellor Kohl's claim of "the grace of late birth," once again stressing his own credentials as a sophisticated rememberer.[8] The flexible situational dynamic is also visible in an aside by his classmate just before I left, after I had expressed surprise at how oppressive this history was for them. He said, "I shouldn't worry since they don't really feel bad. It is just in the museum that this is expected" (Field diary from 13 September 2007). This later positioning, in my reading, is not a contradiction of the previous ones. Rather, it shows that minute one of an encounter brings about a very particular performance, as in making a good first impression, while after time the situation develops; other performances and functions emerge, such as the one meant to spare my worrying. This does, however, illustrate the ease and proficiency with which these young men navigated the topic, fulfilling an implicit requirement for affective engagement with the museum (cf. Bishop Kendzia 2012: 81–82).

In a subsequent group interview, one young man, who had conducted his visit as a memorial activity but also spent a lot of time in the Rafael Roth Learning Center, expressed his disappointment with the museum:

> I personally did not find the Garden of Exile so thrilling. Just like the [Holocaust] Memorial. It does not do much for me. Rather … well, I had the fear that it would be more or less an exhibition about the Holocaust. And it was more or less just this, especially in the underground levels. And then one floor higher with this white room that led to the masks—well, I don't know. I would have preferred it, if the Holocaust had been left out altogether and more about the history of Jewry had been displayed. The way it was, the Holocaust took up almost half the exhibition, which I found was a bit of a pity. (TR 4 group interview 17 September 2007: 5)

The suggestion of leaving the Holocaust out altogether in a Jewish Museum anywhere, let alone in Germany, struck me as remarkable and even unthinkable just a few years ago.[9] Still his explanation and a similar one hinted at by his classmate are telling, "I was very impressed with the architecture. I also experienced this depressing feeling—in the Holocaust Tower it was totally cramped. It was also like this in the [Holocaust] Memorial, pretty cramped. I found it, well, very one sided. We already have so much of this. We have this Memorial with the Information Center" (TR 4 group interview 17 September 2007: 4). These replies do indeed point to a saturation with this way of remembering even by those with an expressed commitment to it. The latter specifically mentioned the Holocaust Memorial as being similar to the JMB and wished for something more.

More Than a Holocaust Museum—Visitors in the Upper Floors

While it is clear that for the most part these young visitors detailed above experienced the JMB as primarily a Holocaust Museum (albeit one with a Jewish History Department),[10] the main exhibition on the upper floors seemed to offer a break from this memorial activity.[11] Let us rejoin our group of 11 September 2007 again at the point when they first enter the permanent exhibition after the long climb up the stairs.

Upstairs the mood becomes more relaxed at once. The body language changes—arms moving freely, less at the sides, not across the chest. They quickly approach the Wish Tree, which is just inside the entrance … a few put wishes on the wish tree. One reads the wishes that are already hanging there.

Some watch the film about the beginnings of Jewish settlement in Germany. They sit and watch intently, and they watch the entire show. After this, a few take turns handling the huge garlic clove. They open and close it and read the signage written on it. A little ways further on, we come to a tour in progress. The guide is quite loud and very animated. We all stop to listen. He is doing a sort of interactive tour asking the participants questions and then explaining, for example, the origins of the idea that it was the Jews who killed Christ. This young man is in fact very engaging, and we all want to hear more. I was also taken by this guide's rather adversarial approach. He was explaining and thematizing anti-Semitism as very directly linked to Christendom in some detail, something I found, personally, that the exhibition alone largely glossed over.[12]

After a while of listening to this engaging guide, we go to the next section, Glikl bas Juda Leib . A few of the young women spend a long time here, especially at the big wheel and the suitcase-packing video game. This is an interactive terminal, which asks the visitor to take on the role of Glikl (a merchant woman from seventeenth-century Hamburg) and try to pack the on-screen bag correctly with all the items she would need on her trade journey [see Figure 3.8]. I have tried this several times and have yet to get it right. They seem to be having fun. I overhear one of the young women say, "It's much nicer up here." In the Children's World section, a group of women becomes more animated. They laugh and chat and take turns looking in the camera-like display there. Next the group proceeds to the Nazi era section. They skim it quietly, respectfully. The body language, however, becomes rigid once again: the young men have their arms at their sides, while the young women have them crossed in front of their chests. The group also misses the room with post-1945 and present-day Jews (Field diary 11 September 2007).

It looks like certain interactive elements seemed to act as what I have termed "relaxation spaces," especially after the more hushed and memorial-like atmosphere of the underground axes. Note the fun at playing the packing game, and the evident enjoyment at the Wish Tree and the Children's World.

Let us now return to our group of 7 November 2007, to see how they navigated the upper floors.

Enjoying/Consuming the Interactives

They spend time often at the interactive sections, films, and also some time at the memorial books. The further away they were in time and space from the underground sections, the more relaxed the mood became. The body language reflects this mood, with arms loosely at sides and also in motion, heads up, generally "bewegungsfreudig" (seem delighted to move). The conversation became normal (not hushed). They showed interest most of all at visual, audio, and other interactive spots. The young women were also especially interested in aspects of Jewish daily life (family life, kosher meals, clothing). Three young women are chatting quietly, and when they notice me, they include me: "We like the things here that we can do ourselves." In the next session (Glikl bas Juda Leib), a few linger a while. The mood is calm, respectful but certainly not as solemn as below. The conversation is louder now as they play the computer packing game. This is consistently a hit and occupies a lot of the visitors' time. They also seem to have trouble finding the correct items to pack, as I had.

I notice a group of five eating something. I wonder what it is. I ask them. "They are kosher gummy bears," the young man with the pack in his hand replies. He shows me the pack. He offers me one. I decline. He says the gummy bears taste just the same as "normal" ones, and that they are also like a souvenir because they're "kosher." I note the ambivalence here: kosher gummy bears—a familiar yet exotic snack break—an edible souvenir? (Field diary 7 November 2007).

From the questionnaire replies and interviews of both groups, there is a general consensus that the upper floors were more pleasant and inviting. They were a welcome change from the underground sections. Peleikis and Feldman note that catchy products like these gummy bears are presented in a deliberately accessible way, very attractive to kids (Peleikis and Feldman 2013: 315). Indeed, these young men and women were happily eating them. For example, one young woman wrote of the upper floors, "What with the delightful color, I felt somewhat better and more secure" (QR 28, R 2.4). And another noted the contrast more explicitly: "It was fun to discover things and in contrast to the underground section I felt good, and with the Wish Tree, for example, I felt good, and somehow integrated" (QR 29, R 2.4). While this was elaborated on as follows in the group interview, "I also thought—I don't know if the architect had this in mind—that in the underground section, one is confronted with the horrible things that happened: and in the upper section, the way it was, one was received rather as a human being with this tree and the warm, friendly atmosphere. So there was a contrast between below and above ground there" (TR 3 group interview 13 September 2007: 2).

I do find the choice of language here significant. Down in the axes one is "confronted with the horror." While upstairs one is greeted "rather as a human being." This implies something dehumanizing in her perception of the experiences below, not to mention the reading of the Kadishman installation, treated above, where she (this is the same young woman) felt compelled to take on a perpetrator role.

The suggestion that such experiences might be alienating is important, especially for empathizing on the issue of Holocaust fatigue and subsequent avoidance of the topic. What follows is an illustration of a strong desire to focus on something other than the Holocaust on the part of teachers and students coupled with a strategy the visitors used to accomplish this in situ.

An Ethnographic Snapshot: A Teacher's Perspective

On a visit with this group,[13] *I meet the teacher who will accompany us to the museum. She explains that she has to come with us and take attendance to make sure everyone gets to the museum. She is friendly and at the museum asks me about my work, and mentions what she most likes about this museum: it is not only about the Holocaust. That is its great strength. Her students are fed up of the Holocaust and want more, and this museum offers that* (Field diary 2 July 2007).

From this brief interaction, I infer two things: that the message of the JMB not being a Holocaust museum is getting across to an important audience, this high school teacher and probably others too. Second, that

Holocaust fatigue is something that is common knowledge in her experience as a teacher and is something she has to contend with in their work.

It is in this context of Holocaust fatigue and attempts to counter it then that I think one can best situate this disconnect between the lower and upper floors. A perception of a contrast between the underground axes and the permanent exhibition was evident in much of the material gathered throughout my study. It was during one particular visit, however, with a group of first-time visitors that the contrast was most pronounced. This in turn had implications for the flexible nature of the occasion and the agency of these visitors.

From Avoiding the Museum to Circumventing the Holocaust Memorial Experience

Here I would like to describe the events at some length. We begin in the classroom and then meet up again during the subsequent visits.

I am in a high school in a middle-class area of central Berlin, which was once in the former East. I am here to introduce myself and the project to this grade thirteen history class. The teacher, Mr F., chats with me cordially. He explains that, as a rule in the school, grade thirteen students cannot undertake field trips during school time, as their study schedule is too demanding. Consequently, participation in this project would have to take place after school hours. When I ask the class who might want to take part in the study, several hands go up. Then we discuss possible dates. In this, the teacher helps out. He notes two dates on the blackboard, and those who would like to take part sign up. Not all can make it on the same day, but a number would indeed like to take part. So I say it is fine to have two visits, even two small groups, to accommodate their schedules. We agree on two dates, and I collect e-mail contact details so that I can confirm their coming and get in touch should any problems arise. I have two sign-up lists. There are six scheduled for the first meeting and eight for the second. The students make an interested, mature impression on me.

This will be an interesting contrast to the other visits, I think; here all the participants would be going on their own time and would not then "get a day off school" for this trip (Field diary 20 September 2007).

Three days later, I receive the following e-mail from one of the young women who had signed up to come. (I have taken out her name, and that of her school, replaced it with initials that do not match the originals, but I have kept the font and size the same.)

hello
my name is n.s. from a.l. gymnasium.

i was going to go to the jüdischem museum with you, but unfortunately i have to cancel the excursion.
ive been there a few times before and it is an amazing museum, but it always depresses me to go there …
i thought i was stronger and therefore wanted to go with you … but i think its better if i dont …
i hope you understand!
im really sorry
kind regards
n.

Many things go through my mind at this point. First, how nice that she actually bothered to excuse herself. Then I wonder why she felt the need to explain herself? Then I think: wow a reason not to want to go is important too: that it makes her depressed. I reply and ask if she would mind telling me more, but she does not reply to me and I leave it at that. It is interesting that she said she has been there a few times already and is always sad after. I wonder how her classmates will take the museum (Field diary 23 September 2007).

A group of five students arrives, and we begin our visit together. In the axes, they look at some of the displays and begin to read the personal stories beside the artifacts in the cabinets embedded in the walls. They all take the time to read several stories. This continues also in the Axis of Exile. They spend a few minutes just in the axes, reading, looking, not talking.

We come to the Holocaust Tower. Two of the young women lead us there, in fact. Here they do not seem to want me to lead them. They want to find their own way. At times, though, they do ask me questions. One points to the door to the tower and asks, "What's that? What's supposed to happen there?" I explain that it is called the Holocaust Tower and that it is often perceived as an "Erinnerungsort" (a memorial place), but is open to other interpretations. (This is the explanation that I have most often heard from museum staff, and I do not want to misrepresent the structure.) I ask the group if they want to go inside and see. They do. I open the door, and we enter. They are silent, noticeably so. Then two whisper, "stifling" and "It's painful here," respectively. One of the women seems nervous and tries to suppress something: (a shudder, perhaps, I can't tell exactly). Then another goes to the door and knocks on it. She turns to me: "I want out!," she says, again in a whisper. She had knocked on the door to be "let out." In fact, they all wanted to leave and thought too that they had to wait. I open the door, and we all exit. No attendant is there. In all we spent maybe less than two minutes in the tower. We walk back down the Axis of the Holocaust and proceed along the Axis of Exile to the garden beyond it. They walk along the columns, and one woman asks her classmate, "What's this supposed to mean?" She replies, "It's like the Holocaust Memorial. You're supposed to feel afraid and be quiet." It occurs to me that they seem then to read this section of the museum through their previous experience of the HM with its waving field of stelae. They walk slowly but deliberately among the columns for a minute or two. Then they go inside again. In total, we spend less than fifteen minutes in the underground sections.

We enter the upper section, and the relief is immediately palpable. One young woman says in an almost gasping tone, "Oh, it's much nicer here!" The mood goes from the somber one that was present downstairs and the cautious one as they mounted the long black staircase, to a relaxed one. The body language changes too. They seem to breathe out (as if they had been holding their breath a little before). In this moment, I am reminded of a funeral of a close family member I had recently attended and found the mood eerily similar. First, the solemn ceremony, then the happier wake with coffee and cake.

They go straight to the Wish Tree, and three write wishes. We walk through the museum, and they intermittently handle interactive displays throughout, watching, listening, laughing. In the "Glikl" section, they comment on the wheel, which they operate, and the packing video game, which they play several times. We move on to the section dedicated to the Nazi era. The mood changes again here. It becomes very solemn, silent. Next, and to my surprise, they do find the green room dedicated to present-day Jews in Germany. They are much more relaxed here and smile. They spend some time listening to several of the stories (Field diary 26 September 2007).

Another small group, from the same class, visits the following evening.

It is raining a bit this late afternoon, and I am waiting outside the main entrance of the museum. The group arrives, and they smile as they recognize me. I say hello and ask whether they have been to the museum before. One young woman replies: No, none of us has been before, but they have heard a lot about the museum and are eager to see it. I ask what they had heard: "That it's impressive, especially the architecture," is the reply.

In the axes, their body language is reserved much like the other visitors present at the time. Their faces are expressionless as they look at the side panels, read them, and read the texts along the walls, arms crossed across the chest. One mentions how "slanted" the floors are here. We come to the Holocaust Tower, and this time an attendant opens the door as we approach. We enter. They are silent. They look up, one leaves after a few seconds as soon as the door is opened from the outside. The others follow soon thereafter. They also do visit the Garden of Exile, walk carefully among the columns for a short time, and then tell me that they would like to see the exhibition upstairs now.

On the way up the stairs, one young woman remarks, "One sees what a difference the architecture makes!" Upon entering the space on the second upper level, one young woman exclaims, "Oh, a tree!" They smile at each other and me, and start to chat with one another, "What is one supposed to do there?" But the answer becomes self-evident: they go to the counter and fill out wishes on the paper pomegranate cutouts. They spend quite some time here handling things (wooden bowls, the huge garlic clove, opening drawers). Two young women spend a lot of time at the writing-in-Hebrew terminal. They wrote their own names as well as a number of other words such as, "Ashkenas," for example. Generally, the group moves cheerfully through the permanent exhibition, seems relaxed, talks, and laughs together. One puts on a headphone set and laughs loudly at what she hears. She smiles at me and says, "It's funny here with the movies and kids explaining things." (She is referring to the headphones she had just put down.) The group spends at least fifteen minutes at this table alone, listening in turn and laughing, talking about it with each other.

As we pass two statues along the side in the Moses Mendelssohn section, one young woman asks me, "Were they so small?" I look at the statues more closely. I had never really given them much attention, and the question came at me unexpectedly. I walk up to one and see that it is indeed very small. They do not appear life-sized to me, I say. I note that her question shows an expectation that the museum might have accurate facsimiles or authentic representations. In the next section, they continue to converse light-heartedly about the exhibits. The one about kosher food gets their attention, and they spend some time here. They remark to each other and to me, commenting in an amused tone about how complicated it would be to have to keep the milk and meat dishes apart, "They had two sets of dishes for this!" They had also earlier expressed wonder at how many children Glikl bas Juda Leib had had (fourteen!). They go through the next sections more quickly and cheerfully, but stop at the Nazi era section that begins with the signage, "Persecution, Resistance, Extermination." Here, the body language is once again rigid, and arms go up again crossed against the chest as they read the signage about the persecution of the Jews. They spend very little time here and do not talk at all.

After this, looking a bit lost, two ask me if there is anything else to see. I mention two more sections, one on postwar to present-day Jewish life in Germany, nearby, and the Kadishman installation. This group wants to see the Kadishman installation and would rather skip the present-day section. So I take them to this. They have spent over two and a half hours in the upper sections and are now getting tired. We finish the visit at the Kadishman instal-lation which, after reading the sign, they do carefully walk over (Field diary 17 September 2007).

Going over these two visits, certain characteristics stand out sharply: the very stark contrast between the expressed mood in the lower and upper floors, including the disproportionate amount of time spent in both: very little in the underground sections, very much in the permanent exhibition. Thinking about this in terms of occasioned behavior, recalling Goffman's assertion that "the same physical space may be caught within the domain of different social occasions" (Goffman 1963: 20), I read these visits as examples of visitors actively endeavoring to change the occasion. That is to alter it from a potentially depressing one (remember their classmate's indicated reason for cancellation) to a more pleasant one.

The young women accomplished this by cutting short the time and engagement dedicated to the underground sections with their strong Holocaust memorial-like atmosphere, choosing rather to spend much time and involvement exploring the permanent exhibition. Here, I think it is fair to characterize these visits then as much more a touristic leisure activity (as in MacCannell 1976: 34–35) than a memorial activity. Indeed, they were not so much a continuation of school "work." Remember too that these two visits were the only ones conducted outside of school time.

Additionally, the fascination at the quaint kosher dinner service and the question asking if they—the Jews—had been so small, points to another problematic issue that surrounds visitors' perceptions of the museum exhibitions. Namely, the practice of presenting Jews as exoticized others. This reinforces a clichéd narrative of Jews, not only as victims, but also as a lost, exotic people of the past (Bishop Kendzia 2010: 54). This effect serves to reinforce hard boundaries between Jews and non-Jews, further rendering the dominant culture of memory, and Germanness for that matter, inaccessible to Jews, for example.

Reviewing the pre- and post-visit questionnaire replies from this group also makes the contrast between the underground sections and the upper floors quite clear. They all noted a lot of background knowledge on the topic in the home and in their own free time. Moreover, they associated very negative feelings with it. One of the young women whose engagement in the museum was predominantly one of fun and play, had, prior to the visit, noted, "Sadness, anger, shame. What happened in the past is terrible. Yet there are still neo-Nazis in Germany today. There are parties like the NPD [a far right German nationalist political party], and Synagogues need police protection today. This makes me sad" (QR 51, R 1.11). But, after her visit, she wrote the following, "I didn't think that the visit could be such fun … Although the topic of the exhibitions is, naturally, a serious one, I could laugh a lot. It was very interesting. Now, I also connect positive feelings with Jewish history in Germany" (QR 51, R 2.2, 2.4, 2.8). Further, she indicated that she thought she would most remember, "The kids who explained what Judaism was" (QR 51, R 2.10). This refers directly to the experience in the museum when she laughed aloud and included her classmates and myself in the conversation.

Another from her class, who had visited the day before, gave the following pre- and post-visit replies:

> I am very sensitive when it comes to racist remarks. And, I am ashamed as a German for the people who have not yet learned and are racists (QR 47, R 1.11). [Now after the visit:] The cabarets that one could see were very amusing, and so did not initially fit with my image of the Jewish Museum. After thinking about it briefly, though, I think it did, in fact, work. The Jews were shown from a side that one hardly thinks about today (QR 47, R 2.2). … I have never thought about the time when they could live free and easily, and I think it's good that this side also gets shown. (QR 47, R 2.7)

Further reflecting her visiting practices in the museum, she indicated that what she would likely most remember was "the kosher food, my name in Hebrew" (QR 47, R 2.10).

It seems from these replies that the vast majority of these young visitors' previous knowledge about the topic of Jewish history was centered firmly and exclusively on the Holocaust. The museum could offer a departure from this for them, provided that they actively partook of this opportunity. The replies to what they would most remember are indeed remarkable as they were among the very few in the study that did not emphasize Holocaust memorial-related elements. Choosing to focus on "the kids explaining Judaism," and the time when "Jews could live free and easily" also points to another type of remembering activity that itself highlights a happier Jewish situation/past in Germany. Feldman and Peleikis (2014) point out that such display practices "dissipate the museum object as sacra and nullify the effect of the voids" (Feldman and Peleikis 2014: 49). This is clearly the case here. Further, it is a nullification that the visitors actively sought out. Y Michal Bodemann argues that such happy representations, of a pre-1933 German-Jewish past fulfill a sort of ideological labor for the German, non-Jewish mainstream and their meaning-seeking needs, conjuring up an idealized, glorious past (Bodemann 1996: 50). Above, they offer an alternative to focusing on Holocaust memory, with which these young visitors have already been saturated.

Let us return now to the young woman, who had written to me to cancel her participation. I have mentioned John Dewey as informing some of my implicit ideas on education. His very pragmatic approach to "educative experience" helps me to position situations such as the one here. Dewey argues:

> The belief that all genuine education comes about through experience does not mean that all experiences are genuinely or equally educative. Experience and ed-

> ucation cannot be directly equated to each other. For some experiences are mis-educative. Any experience is mis-educative that has the effect of arresting or distorting the growth of further experience … it may produce lack of sensitivity and responsiveness. Then the possibilities of having richer experiences in the future are restricted. (Dewey 1938, 1998: 13)

Might not the situation with the young woman who cancelled be indicative of miseducative experiences with this topic? Ones that have led to such a fatigue with it that further involvement is avoided. Creative agency—altering the occasion—may mitigate this and even make for an "educative experience" in the museum. The impulse to avoid or circumvent, nevertheless, remains. I too wonder at the issue of degree of negative feelings. How much is too much to render an experience miseducative? Let us return for a moment to Dean MacCannell, who writing on cultural experiences as being fundamental to maintaining morality, notes, "The 'uplifting' experience … can arise from the dramatic representation of the darkest and most threatening of crimes" (MacCannell 1976: 27–28). While this can indeed be the case, I would argue that in the situations here, the way in which this dark Nazi past is being remembered has resulted in a negation of the uplifting experience. This memorialization is, of course, not limited to the museum, or the activity of visiting it or other similar sights, but a process and a habitus that is longer term and plurilocal.

Unstable Spaces: Situational Factors

I mentioned earlier that I hesitate to fully apply Stuart Hall's model, as the situations are indeed varied, and not nearly as static and clear-cut as the *code* categories might suggest. Here I would like to elaborate briefly on the limitations of these categories in terms of approaching the ethnographic material. Just to recap, in addition to perceiving messages according to a *dominant code,* Hall describes some consumers of media as reading messages according to *negotiated codes* (1980: 137; not quite what the producers had in mind) and puts this up to misunderstandings and failures to communicate, and finally, *oppositional codes,* which he characterizes as deliberate contrary readings (Hall 1980: 138). I have come to find that a too strict lens misses the blurry spaces in between. I had been struggling with some difficult material. A few visitors who had indicated reading parts of the museum indeed as the producers might well have expected. They showed solemn respect in terms of body language in the underground sections, expressed feelings of fear and empathy in the Holocaust Tower, and had been exposed to this topic outside of school—reading Anne Frank, visiting other memorial sites and former concentration camps. They then went on to express what appeared to be either negotiated or even oppositional readings of other sections. I refer here to a few replies on the questionnaires by these otherwise very solemn visitors indicating that they felt "very happy and free" in the Garden of Exile and remember it as an "enjoyable space" in which they felt "liberated" (QR 26, 29, 48). This occurred at a time when the signage upon entering the garden asked that one try to imagine the unsettling sense of disorientation that exile brings. The experience was meant to be jarring, not comfortable, I thought.[14] Indeed, the vast majority of their classmates indicated such a reading: noting feelings of being lost, confused, insecure, and even frightened.

It was only after going over my field notes for the days in question (11 September 2007 and 7 November 2007) that I could put these puzzling replies into context. A few of the young visitors on both days had been part of small groups who had just a few minutes prior to visiting the Garden of Exile been literally trapped in the Holocaust Tower—or thought they were. They had thought that they could only leave the tower when a staff member opened the door.[15] In one case, I was with them, and I opened the door, after one of the young women whimpered to be let out. In the other, the attendant left after they remained inside for quite some time. No wonder some from this group then felt free outside in the Garden of Exile! This was neither a negotiated nor an oppositional reading; it was rather a situational-reactional reading. It resulted from the unpredictable dynamics of the situation. While Hall's categories are indeed helpful, they do not suffice—perhaps are too static—to account for all the processes at play in meaning making. I aim to delve deeper and recognize that readings too are dynamic rather than static and can be influenced by a myriad of situational factors. At the same time, ignoring the framework of the dominant discourse and its mechanisms of exclusion would be irresponsible and render the differences banal as if they were inconsequential (cf. Kirshenblatt-Gimblett 1998: 243), which, as we shall see, they are not.

Notes

1. (Cf. Till 2005: 167). Such sentiments also were widely reported in the press at the time.
2. Dean MacCannell's contributions come up again in the next chapter. What I would like to emphasize here is the difficulty of binaries: either touristic or memorial. It seems to be a question of degree, as in more or less memorial or more or less touristic. Another point is that I use the term touristic first as a

descriptor in order to distinguish it from memorial activity. I do not attach a negative or derisive value to it (cf. MacCannell 1976: 94), although some readers may do this. I do believe that I should keep the term "tourist" as it is clear, in Chapter 4, which I entitle: "The Visit as a Predominantly Touristic Activity" that this term is indeed entirely fitting as a comparative one.

3. This culturally monolithic makeup struck me immediately. I was still surprised by the "whiteness" of this class. I did expect much more mixing to be evident in Berlin schools. After all, I had been living in Berlin (first Kreuzberg, then South Neukölln) not too far away from the school these visitors attend. I just falsely assumed the schools would reflect the local population in a more even way. Little did I know then how segregated the schools in Berlin, in fact, are, even in areas like Kreuzberg with a majority population with immigrant background. When I started this research, my own children were not yet in school. Now, however, they are, and I am still dumbstruck by the horror expressed quite regularly by parents of acquaintances of my elder daughter's when I mention which school she attends: "Oh, but there are so many 'migrants' in that school." "Yes" I say, "My daughter will fit right in." This usually results in a confused look and more often than not a comment to the tone of: "No, I don't mean you. You are not a migrant." In the case of her school, it is only about 20 percent "children of migrant background," and the quality of education is very high. Still, fear of this 20 percent is, at times, enough to send many others looking for "more German" schools.

4. For an exploration of the prevalence of this reading of the museum experience, see Bishop Kendzia 2010.

5. A desire to avoid a misplaced and misleading pseudo-psychoanalytic approach is hardly new, which is problematic even when analyzing individual behavior (I am not a trained psychologist), and all the more inappropriate in looking at group activities. This stance is something I share with other scholars (cf. Kansteiner 2002; Young 1993: xi).

6. Dean MacCannell also recognized this difficulty, arguing that it is not possible to "make facile distinctions between mere acts and authentic expressions of true characteristics. In places where tourists gather, the issues are even more complex" (MacCannell 1976: 95–96). Indeed, the key role of place, the JMB as a particular sight and field site, is all the more crucial to positioning the performances. Scott and Selwyn (2010: xviii) also ask important questions regarding sincerity and authenticity at tourist sites, where performances are "amplified": if most behavior was "performed authenticity" what counts as "genuine" and "sincere"? These questions further unsettle any simple binaries of true and untrue (Bishop Kendzia 2014: 61–62).

7. So-Sein/So-Erscheinen-Wollen.

8. On 25 January 1984, Chancellor Helmut Kohl held a speech in the Israeli Knesset, in which he characterized himself as "someone who was free from guilt, because he benefited from the grace of late birth" (als einer, der in der Nazizeit nicht in Schuld geraten konnte, weil er die Gnade der späten Geburt

… hat). This statement caused much controversy at the time and has been referred to repeatedly over the years in the public domain.

9. Robin Ostow (2007: 310) recalls that all Jewish museums in Europe feature a major Holocaust installation.
10. Cf. Bishop Kendzia 2010.
11. Cf. Bishop Kendzia 2011.
12. Gudehus 2002 also had a similar impression that anti-Semitism remained largely unexplained.
13. This is from a visit, with a group from a part of former West Berlin, a largely lower class area. The participants were children of former West Germans.
14. At the time, the signage specifically instructed visitors to think about the disorientation that exile brings. I understood this to mean one should feel insecure and upset. Since then, however, guides on a number of JMB tours, I have been part of, temper this aspect, saying you can feel whatever you want. It is meant to be ambiguous and unsettling.
15. The belief that they had to be let out of the Holocaust Tower was not an unusual one among the visitors in my study as I have already illustrated. I return to this confusion in Chapter 5 and have also explored it further in Bishop Kendzia 2012.

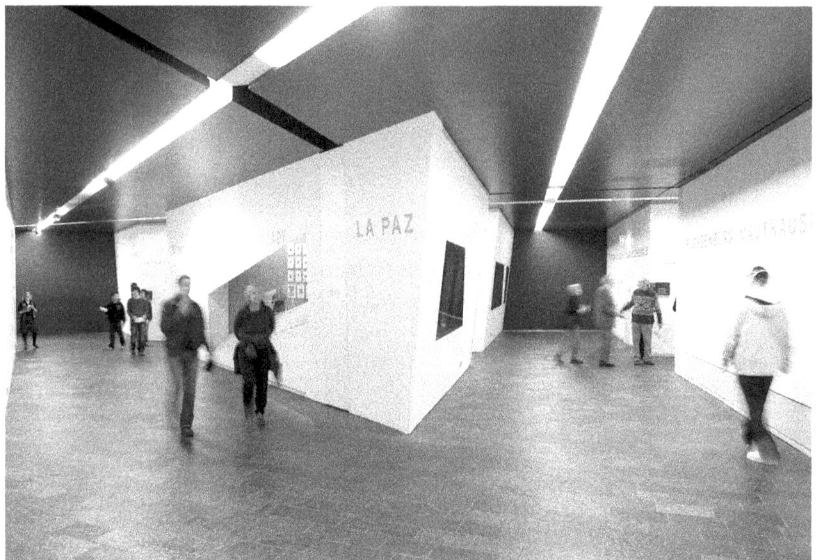

Fig 3.1 Underground Axes (Jewish Museum Berlin, photo: Thomas Bruns)

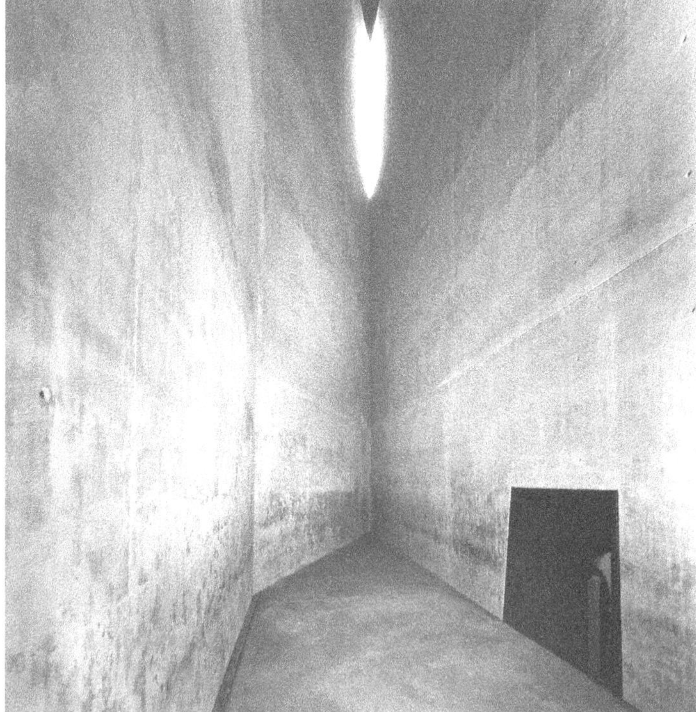

Fig 3.2 The Holocaust Tower (Jewish Museum Berlin, photo: Jens Ziehe)

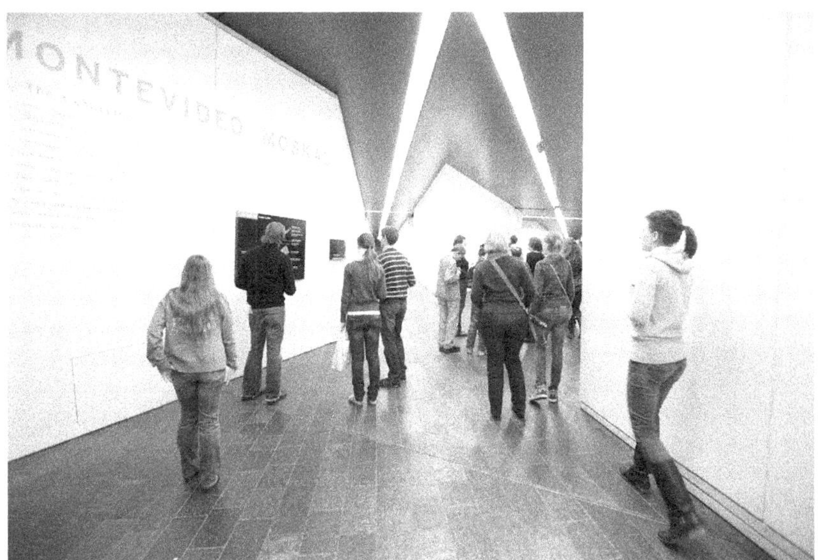

Fig 3.3 The Axis of Exile (Jewish Museum Berlin, photo: Ernst Fesseler)

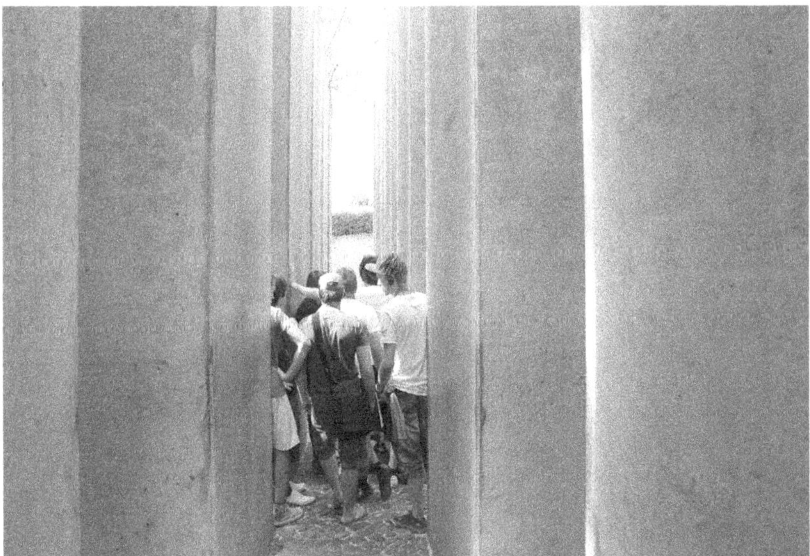

Fig 3.4 The Garden of Exile (Jewish Museum Berlin, photo: Ernst Fesseler)

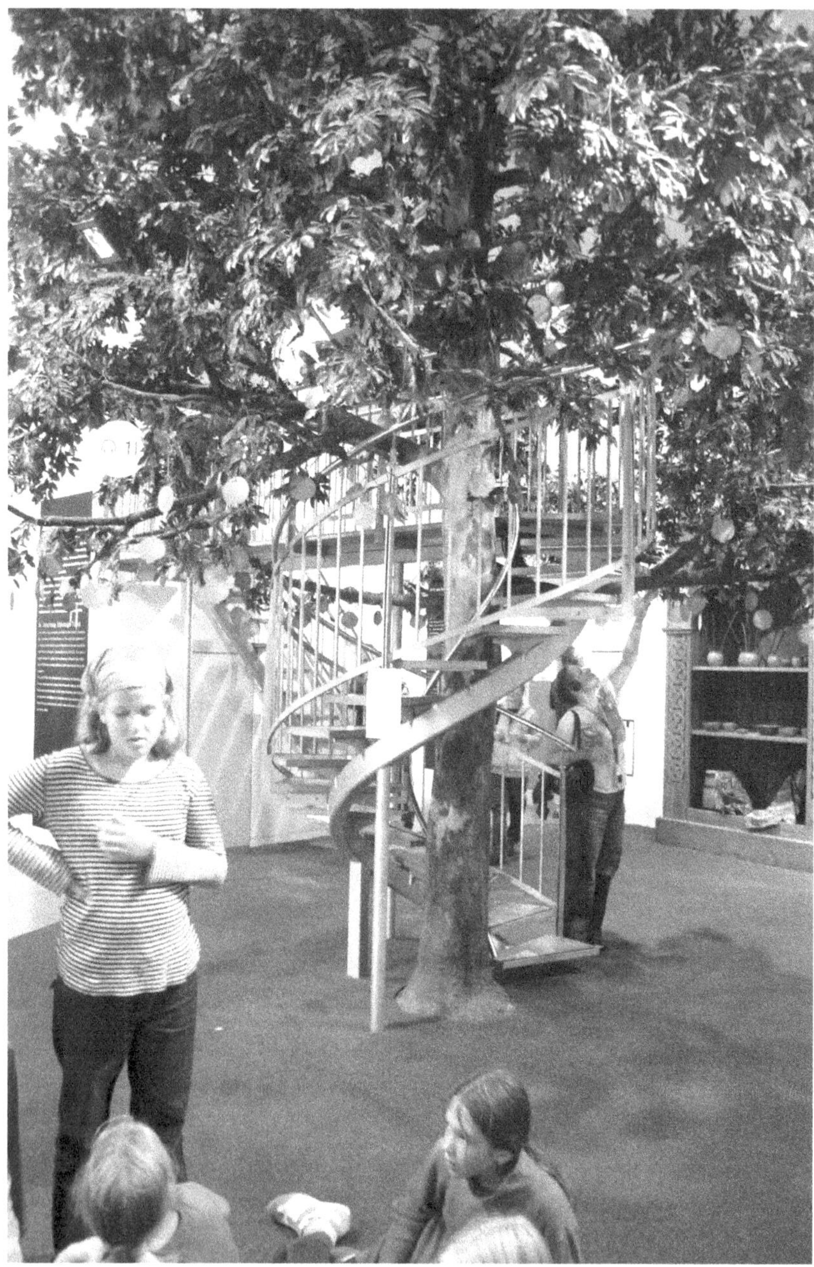

Fig 3.5 The Wish Tree (Jewish Museum Berlin, photo: Sybille Büttner)

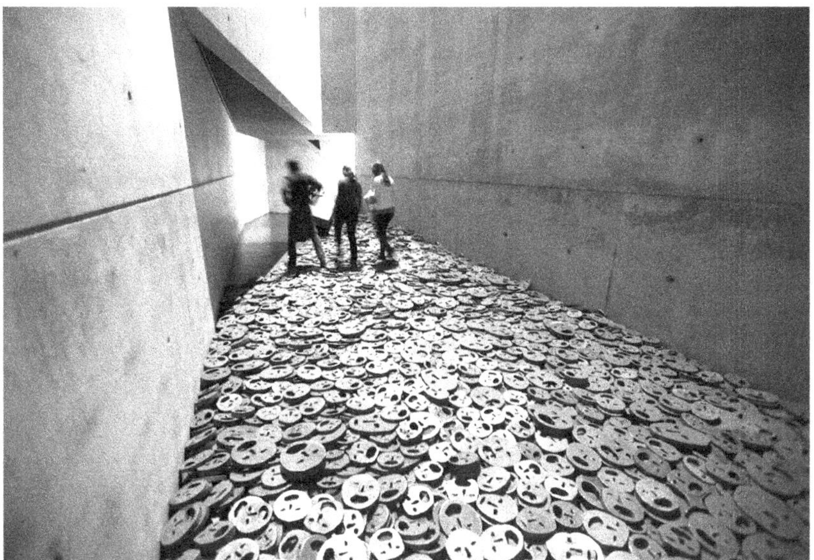

Fig 3.6 *Fallen Leaves* installation by Menashe Kadishman (Jewish Museum Berlin, photo: Ernst Fesseler)

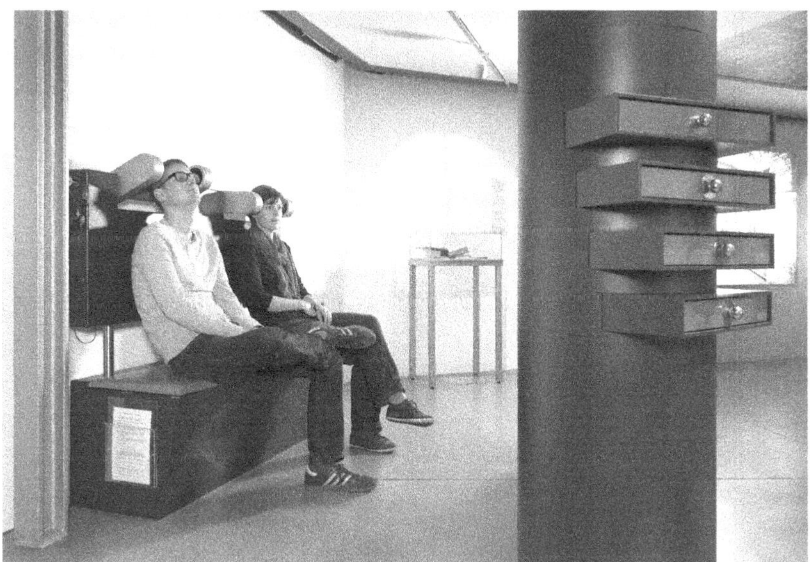

Fig 3.7 Interactive section on horse trading (Jewish Museum Berlin, photo: Jens Ziehe)

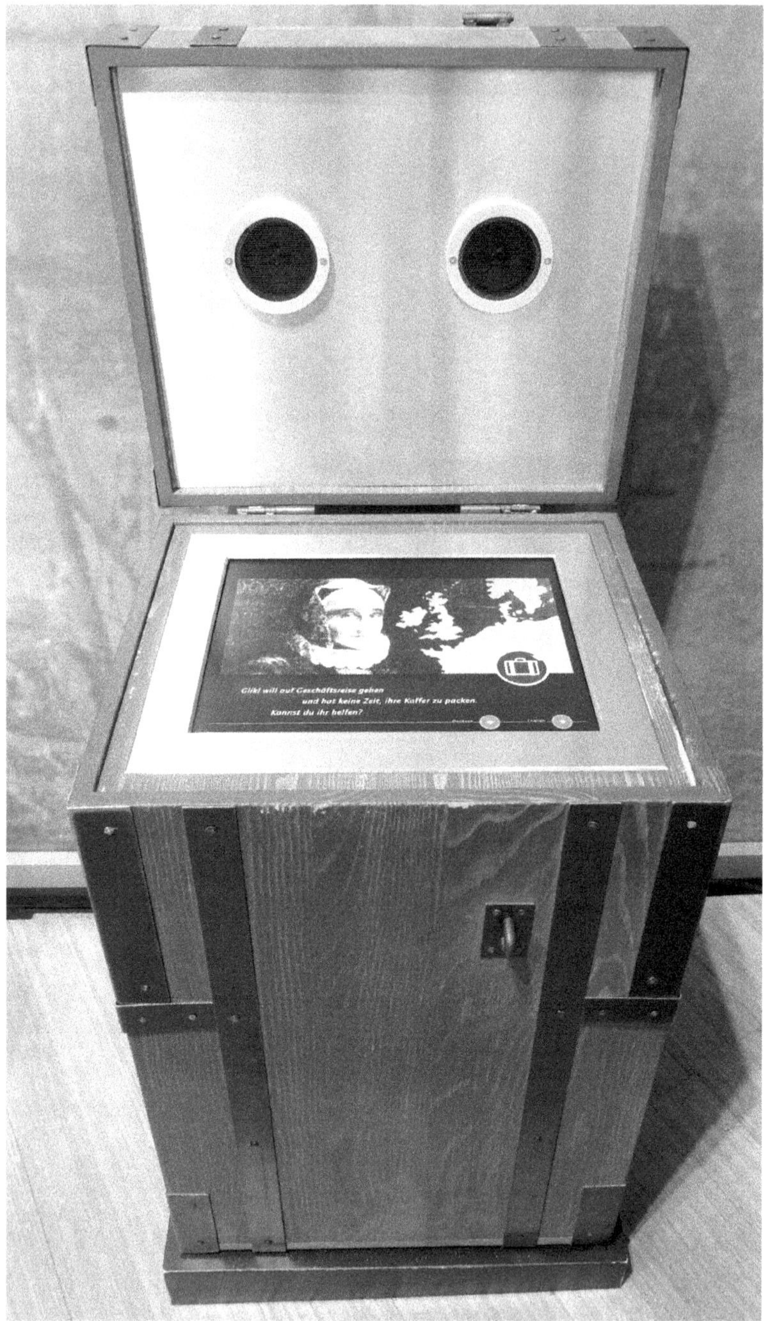

Fig 3.8 Suitcase-packing interactive game (Jewish Museum Berlin, photo: Jens Ziehe)

Chapter 4

The Visit as a Predominantly "Touristic" Activity

Reflections on Tourism and Authenticity

That the JMB is a tourist site and sight is hardly a new discovery as the visitor figures already mentioned demonstrate. Indeed, many of the visitors in my own study also commented on this aspect. Let us recall that the term "tourist" is often not merely a neutral descriptor. A conversation with a fellow student at my institute just before I embarked on my research comes to mind and illustrates the tensions evident in understandings of this term. I had mentioned that I wanted to do research at the JMB, and he commented, in my mind somewhat dismissively, even waving his hand as if to push my idea aside: "Why at such a *touristic* place. Why not somewhere more *authentic*?" The derision was clearly audible in his emphasis of the word "*touristic*." He nearly spat it out (Field diary 16 May 2006). I am reminded here of the continued relevance of MacCannell's assertion that: "The term 'tourist' is increasingly used as a derisive label for someone who seems content with his obviously inauthentic experiences" (MacCannell 1976: 94).[1] Similar sentiments were later expressed by young men of upper–middle class West German background in my study, especially in the form of shock at, and disapproval of, the commercial aspects of the museum shop (QR 41, R 2.6), for example. This same visitor who disliked the shop also indicated his dissatisfaction with the permanent exhibition:

I thought it was a pity that they tried so compulsively to add variety in the exhibition, for example, with many/unnecessary and in my opinion bad use of media. I would have preferred it, if the exhibits had been more seriously displayed, and not so playfully (QR 41, R 2.4). Since my thirst for knowledge could not be satisfied here, I will inform myself elsewhere. (QR 41, R 2.9)

This episode brings me to another aspect of authenticity, namely its relativity, which is worthy of some consideration, especially in an endeavor to unsettle so-called universals. Very early on in the process, I met with visitor services staff at the JMB sharing short descriptions of my research plans, which I had prepared in German. I had in one line referred to the JMB as a *Gedenkstätte*—as in a "memorial site." I was immediately corrected. The staff member replied to the effect: "No, we only use the term *Gedenkstätte* in German for authentic sites, like former concentration camps: *Gedenkstätte Sachsenhausen,* for example. Nonauthentic memorials, such as the JMB or the Holocaust Memorial (HM) are called variously: *Denkmäler, Mahnmäler, Erinnerungssorte, Erinnerungsräume,* and so on" (Field diary 25 May 2006). All of these words could be translated into "memorial." There appears to be a hierarchy of authenticity at play here then with certain words reserved only for more authentic sites. That from my point of view, all Berlin, and Germany for that matter, could be described as an authentic site does not alter this hierarchy, but does put it into perspective. Perhaps too, the derision of the student at my institute that I encountered early on also reflected an appreciation of this differentiation, as much as it did his disdain for the JMB *per se.* Reflections on the role of authenticity did come up, in a similar way, in the interviews with certain visitors. Here are just two contrasting examples: in a group discussion on the significance of the museum's location, one young man of middle-class West German background expressed the following:

> Well, with now this, with the Jew memorial [Holocaust Memorial], it is, I think, it's become very public, but I would've put it more near an extermination camp, or a former extermination camp and not in Berlin, because Berlin …
> [Here his classmate interrupts] Were you already, how often have you been there?
> –What in Sachsenhausen?
> –Yes.
> –Six, seven times.
> –Woah (laughs). I have only been three times.
> –I was also in Auschwitz … it's really interesting there.
>
> (Here I notice the teacher getting fidgety and seeming quite uncomfortable.) I continue wanting to hear more: You said something, that it should be near an extermination camp, so an authentic site, where something actually happened, but here it is so …
>
> [He continues]: Berlin is such a neutral choice. It's such a neutral point where it is, since it really didn't well, okay granted, with the Prussians like, but it doesn't really … have to do with Germany's formative history, the Holocaust. The decisions were made there, like, but I would still say that it would be more appropriate to have it near an extermination camp or at least close to a former concentration camp. (TR 1 group interview 22 June 2007: 2)

For this young man the JMB was not authentic enough and could have benefitted from being located in a place more directly involved in the relevant history of Germany—for him, as for many other visitors in my study, the relevant history was reduced to the Holocaust. Further, he had been to one former concentration camp seven or eight times and went on to demonstrate a sort of fascination with the topic. It was at this point in the interaction that the teacher became visibly uncomfortable and countered him, effectively silencing him, alluding to his original criticism of the museum's location with: "Well, that makes absolutely no sense at all. The museum does not at all have the aim of teaching about the Holocaust" (TR 1 group interview of 22 June 2007: 3). I have since come across this phenomenon—a figure in a position of power in a situation (in this case the teacher) becoming irritated with any form of fascination with the Nazi past. Viola Georgi (2003), for example expressed such discomfort quite openly when it came up with her interview partners.

In a subsequent interview with another comparable group (also German of West German background, but from more elite circles) again on the topic of the museum's location, the opposite opinion was made quite explicit. Referring to many of the questionnaire replies, I asked:

> Some also wrote that it is important that there is a museum like this in Berlin. That it is politically important. What do you think about this, about a museum like this here in the capital city?
>
> [A young man replies] Yes, where else should it be? I could hardly imagine a museum like this in Bonn or somewhere.
>
> [I continue] I have spoken with some people who said it should be in an authentic place like in a concentration camp or the like.
>
> [He replies] I don't think so. Then the building would be even more emotionally charged, that would be even more fatal. Berlin is indeed authentic. Hitler wanted to build his Germania-Berlin here. So I couldn't think of a better place for it. (TR 4 group interview of 17 September 2007: 2)

These brief episodes do illustrate the instability of authenticity even among groups that might be expected to hold a common understanding of the term. In addition, they point very much to a perception of further roles of the museum: its strong memorial aspect, and its educational potential—which for one of the young men cited earlier, whose "thirst for knowledge" was left unquenched—was not realized (QR 41, R 2.9). Ed Bruner's concept of constructed authenticity (Bruner 2004) is particularly relevant here. Bruner understands authenticity as socially constructed by the beholders in a continuous meaning-making process in the present. It is therefore neither static nor inherent to an object itself. This approach is helpful in exploring the issue here. We can see how the idea of what is authentic shifts according to the viewer. I also see these small conflicts over what is authentic as part of a larger and far-reaching struggle for what in German is termed *Deutungsmacht,* the power to interpret. This power is, of course, at the root of the dominant discourse so central to contextualizing my findings.

Clearly, an understanding that the JMB is also a tourist site, and some appreciation of this, is not lost on many of the visitors. Indeed, the previous chapter has touched on the visit being transformed from "work"— as in a continuation of school—to "leisure" when the young after-school time visitors deliberately avoided the more memorial-like sections. Moreover, the visitor numbers alluded to in Chapter 2 point to this museum being a tourist magnet.

It is with the benefit of quite some hindsight and comparison that I have labeled this chapter: The Visit as a Predominantly "Touristic" Activity. It is a question of degree and not of either/or as at some points along most visits some "touristy" aspects were visible. What is remarkable in the following encounters was the near absence of a memorial experience. This, in turn, exposed assumptions regarding appropriate visitor behavior at the museum. These assumptions remind us that the museum is a stage, where performances are visible to diverse audiences. One of the hallmarks of the GT approach I am taking is constant comparison. It is through comparisons that differences and similarities become visible. And along this journey I have found just such similarities and contrasts in visiting practices most memorable and challenging. In order to retrace the steps I took to come to this point, I would like now to take you back with me and first introduce you to the next group of participants and then to join them in the museum. In an attempt to maintain the mood and context of the encounters, I describe them at some length, before turning to an analysis of the discrete situations therein.

"Yay!" A Field Trip to the JMB!— ## Enthusiasm without *Betroffenheit*

This is the day arranged with the supportive teacher, Ms P., of this Gesamt-schule (comprehensive school) in a lower–middle class part of Berlin that was once in the East. The teacher herself, now near retirement, had also been raised and educated in East Germany. This was the only individual that actually replied directly to one of my original letters. I introduce myself and the proj-

ect directly to the students. It is a grade eleven history class. My husband is with me. Ms P. is obliging, yet quite formal in her manner, as she had been during my first meeting with her. When I mention a visit to the museum to the class, there are quite a few happy shouts of "yay!" coming from the front of the room, especially from twin sisters seated right in front of me. Two young men toward the back groan in displeasure at the prospect. It would seem some are clearly more enthusiastic than others. Ms P. mentions that it will take place, for those interested, on the "Wandertag" (a school day set aside for outings), which means they have to come to school anyway, so should decide if they want to be part of the museum outing or not. I remind them that it is, of course, voluntary.

We also decided logistically, since it was a very large group to split it up into first-time visitors and repeat visitors, which made sense. We also set a tentative date in early December for the group interview (Field diary 12 October 2007).

We had arranged to meet the group of first-time visitors at 9:45 at the main entrance. They come on time. Ms P. does not come. This is a group of ten. I count seven young women, the enthusiastic twins among them, and three young men. I see now that most of the repeat visitors, who will arrive later today, must be young men and also imagine that the groan in the classroom on our first meeting to mean something like: "I've already seen it and don't feel like going again." I also wonder how much of this participation in my study is the teacher's doing. She is interested in the project and the outcomes, and she seems to have her class very much in order. But not all of her students seem particularly interested. But those who do, appear to be very enthusiastic about the museum visit.

As with almost all the other visiting groups, the young men and women separate into their own groups. We enter the museum at the main entrance, go through security. I get the tickets and send the visitors to the cloakroom to drop off clothing and large bags. They fill out the pre-visit questionnaires rather quickly and separately from each other.

One young woman has a camera and asks me if it is okay that she take pictures. "Yes." I say "But without flash." This group seems a bit lost at first and does indeed want to be led. So I go down the steps and they follow. If I stop, they linger, waiting for my cue. I mention that they are free to go wherever they would like to, and I would follow them. Okay, they say, but they still seem a bit lost. They walk with me, keeping pace with me, and I can sense an excited anticipation in the air. Their body language is neither rigid, nor timid or somber. We could be walking into any interesting museum or gallery. As soon as we pass the entrance to the Rafael Roth Learning Center, they all rush in. They are cheerful and noticeably louder than the other visitors. Four young women surround a model of the museum there and talk animatedly about it:

"That's the museum. Oh shit!" Others go to the computer terminals; the young woman with the camera takes several photos. The four who had surrounded the model of the museum are looking excitedly at the displays on the wall, and talking again in a normal voice—not hushed. From quite some distance, I can hear them saying: "Oh cool, the Jews did this!" I am not facing them, and I walk to leave the room for a moment to see where the young men have gone. On my way out of the room, I hear a woman, who I only later realize is a staff member, admonish them in very unfriendly terms: "It is not 'the Jews,' but rather 'Jewry!'" I am a bit shocked at this and do not know what to make of it. So are the young visitors. They come to me immediately and ask me, "What did I do wrong? Why does one have to say "Jewry" and not "Jews"? I said I had no idea. I really hadn't. I have used the word Jew (in English) and Juden (in German) repeatedly in conversations in the museum (albeit not so loudly and animatedly) and have never encountered such a response. But by the time I went to try to find the staff member, she had disappeared. I wanted to ask her what she meant. Later I found another staff member who I thought might be her. The Rafael Roth Learning Center has dim lighting, and I did not actually see the speaker. It wasn't her, but she explained that the word "Juden" is often considered a bad word and maybe the way it was being said offended her fellow staff member's sensibility on the issue. But why Jewery? This she said she too did not understand.

The young women are visibly upset at being scolded, and I immediately feel sad for them, in addition to being bewildered myself, and I perceived a slight dampening in their enthusiasm. But they soon recovered: we continue along the Axis of the Holocaust. One young woman, still walking quickly and animatedly, bombards me with questions. What is this supposed to be down here? Oh, what is in there (indicating the Holocaust Tower)? I tell her its name and explain that it is often seen as a place to commemorate the Holocaust. We enter the tower together. They are quieter inside, whisper words like "spooky" and "krass" (meaning "extreme" in a cool way, in this slang usage). We are the only ones inside and it is cold, so we leave again after a short time.

The group then makes its way upstairs. They actually enter through the first upper floor (not the second, as would be the suggested beginning), so they end up going through the permanent exhibition backward. This happened as the young man in front just went this way, and the rest followed. First, they go quickly through the section on Persecution, Resistance, Extermination; some pause for a moment at the Children's World section. They are loud and doing things, I would describe as "touristy": taking photos of each other and chatting excitedly about the exhibit pieces.

On the way to the Kadishman installation, we pass a white, empty area. One exhibition here must have been taken down, and the next one is not up yet. Note they have missed the section on post-1945 present-day Jewish life altogether. A few also make their way to the Kadishman display through this white empty section. One comments to me, "Hey, we could rent this room for a party with a bar!" and "If only my room was this big!" They ask why the room is empty. Is it supposed to mean something? I reply that I think they are just in between exhibitions. They walk through this space and ask me what is beyond it. I explain it is an artistic installation with metal structures on the floor. "Oh, I hope it isn't too gross!" exclaims the young woman who had expressed interest in renting the space we were walking through.

They are all excited to walk over the installation. One who had read the sign exclaims to her classmate, "Yeah, you're allowed to!" So, they walk over it excitedly, and one takes pictures of this. Much of the visit proceeds like this. Enthusiastic and excited engagement.

The young women who had been part of the conflict over Jews-Jewry approach me. One asks again, "What did I do wrong?" I shrug looking at her feeling a bit helpless in the situation as I was at a loss to give her an answer. She adds, "There is a lot here that I do not understand. I want to know a couple things: What is a Jew? What is a Christian? What is a Muslim?" I sense how eager she and her fellow classmates are to "get this museum," and I try to fill in the gaps they perceive in their knowledge to the best of my ability, happy that I can at least try and help them with these latter questions. I ask them if they had ever been to church. "No, we all have no religion." Then I try to explain these religious categories: you know the Bible has an Old Testament and New Testament. Yes, this they know. I explain that the Old Testament refers to the Jewish religion. It is a Jewish religious text and is also followed by Christians, who believe that Jesus is God and so follow the teaching of the New Testament, which is mostly about Jesus and St. Paul's teachings. Christians believe that Jesus is the son of God, and God too. The Koran I explain is a later text, and it is the religious text of the Islamic religion and I mention the Prophet Moham-med.[2] All three religions share the basic tenets of the Old Testament and believe in the same God. They are momentarily satisfied, but the one remarks, "God, I have a lot to learn and to look up!" She seemed really upset about the Jew-Jewry episode. Then another young woman who was part of the group took me aside and asked, "Why didn't they just convert?" I am, at first, confused. What do you mean just convert? The Jews who Hitler killed, why didn't they convert to avoid death? Oh, I was at a loss again then replied with a question: "What did you cover in school last year on the topic?" Her reply: "The persecution of the Jews during the Nazi time, that they were excluded and murdered" (Field diary 27 November 2007).

This then was how I noted the museum visit, at the time, of those from this class who had not been to the JMB before. I return to the repeat visitors shortly, but first let us look at some of the questionnaire replies and see how the young pupils themselves described their initial impressions of the outing.

Once at home, I read the replies on the pre- and post-visit questionnaires. Here I am struck by the contrast to all the other groups so far: almost all the pupils had expressed that they had "no feelings" when it came to this history, and further they had not indicated ever discussing it in the home, reading any books on the topic, or having seen any films. Just like the young woman who had only covered the topic for a few weeks in school the year before—that was the sum of the sources on this topic that they had indicated. Here I would like to note that there were three out of the twenty-five students from this group, who were children of former East Germans from this lower-class area who did indeed attest a high degree of previous knowledge on the topic, most notably in the home, and feelings like sadness and guilt. Their replies about the visit too were also very much like those of their counterparts of West German background. These exceptions to the rule of this group do indicate that learned habitus is key. This connection between learned habitus and museum visiting practice would have been the main plot of my basic social process (BSP), had I stuck to a traditional use of GT, as opposed to turning to situational analysis. This BSP is still quite visible, but I do feel that the varied situations are much more telling and illustrative of the issues at hand than the BSP alone might have suggested.

These visitors also for the most part expressed purely physical sensations in the museum spaces, cold, or things like confusion or "creepiness." But there were no mentions of emotions as feelings. No sadness, no sympathy, no *Betroffenheit*, no guilt.

Wow I thought: what a contrast! I start to reflect on the correlations: this was a class of children of former East Germans taught by a former East German teacher. They seemed to not have gotten access to the discourse of dismay or the West German culture of memory. This is still visible in their museum visit today—despite the fact that they themselves were born after the fall of wall, and that they were ostensibly taught according to a unified German curriculum. Perhaps the unified curriculum assumed some common knowledge that these young visitors simply did not have. As expressed, for example, in the questions to me toward the end of the visit as to why the Jews did not just convert to avoid the Nazi persecution. I have to speculate here, as I was not in the classroom the year before in grade ten, when they covered the topic. Nevertheless, it seems quite plausible that they learnt about the topic of the Nazi persecution without actually getting an explanation of the racial categorization of Jews under the Nuremberg laws, and thus without the explicit information that there could be no escape via conversion.

In any case, the young women who bombarded me with such questions did not get this message even if it had been part of the curriculum. Schiffauer, et al. (2004) have found that learning the rules that enable someone to function successfully in society, what they term "civil enculturation" is largely implicit in Germany. The authors base this assertion on their empirical research comparing four European schools. The situation in the museum with the young women, who seemed to feel their own gaps in knowledge certainly support Schiffauer and Baumann's findings. The young women had not covered the topic at all in the home. They had never been to church. They had not developed a habitus of memorial visiting. The fact that the persecution of the Jews was covered in school was not enough for them to "get the museum."

Consider the other pupils in my study who also had parents from former East Germany, albeit of upper–middle class social status. They did not have conflicts in the museum and expressed forms of *Betroffenheit,* sadness, anger, or the like. The young women and men of middle-class background had gotten access to the dominant discourse and built some sort of personal connection to this history, where their counterparts in this lower, once working-class, area did not. Clearly, practices cannot be mapped simply onto origin. It seems to me that it was the lack of having covered the topic at all outside of school, which then led to the absence of personal connection. This not having been accustomed to the practice of memorial visiting, perhaps even correlated to never having been in a house of worship (which could be viewed as another sort of memorial space), seems to be a key factor in contextualizing their social group practice of carrying out the visit to the JMB as a largely touristic activity. This, in turn, helps to put the confusion they expressed in the museum into perspective. It was not a memorial occasion for them in the same way it had been for the groups described in the previous chapter. It was much more a touristic occasion complete with cameras and excitement. Indeed, they had not had enough of the topic. They wanted more of it as a means to understand the museum.

Let us now return to Goffman (1963) in thinking of occasioned behavior and the unwritten rules of bodily idiom surrounding them.

> Gatherings have great significance, for it is through these comings together that much of our social life is organized … those who practice a particular involvement idiom are likely to sense that their rules for participating in gatherings are crucial for society's well-being—that these rules are natural, inviolable and fundamentally right. And these people will need some means of defending themselves against the

doubts that are cast on these rules by persons who break them. (Goffman 1963: 234–35)

Perhaps then the offended party saw the animated behavior of this group to be threatening their own understanding of the right way to behave in this space? I would argue further that the conflict in this case seems to be based on a misunderstanding on the nature of the occasion. To return briefly then to Stuart Hall's categories, the reading of the museum by these visitors would be a sort of negotiated code, not quite what the producers may have had in mind, but based on certain misunderstandings and failures to communicate (1980: 137). The pupils with me were doing a tourist visit, the staff expected and assumed that it should be a memorial visit for these young pupils, and this tension was a big part of the conflict. There was no consensus here on the nature of the occasion. I think the bewilderment of the young women suggest that this was not deliberate provocation, but rather a lack of comprehension—a confusion—that something else was expected of them, and of them in particular.

I also now think, and this must remain speculation, that the staff member's outrage at their use of the word *Jew* likely had a lot to do with her perception of their general touristy behavior and animation as inappropriate. She finally pounced on the word *Jew*, as it was something concrete she could criticize. It might have been too strange for her to directly say: "Stop having so much fun! You are supposed to be moved!" Her strategy is not unlike the teacher's reaction to his pupil's fascination with the Nazi death camps, which took the form of his harsh negation of the young man's perception of the JMB as a Holocaust site (a perception that the vast majority of the participants in my study shared!), rather than a direct attack on fascination, per se. These, my interpretations, of these situations are a sort of intuitive "reading between the lines" based on the dynamic of the situations themselves. The staff member at the JMB finally scolded the group over the use of the word "Jew," but the general touristy behavior throughout seemed to bother not only her, but also others. This came up in later replies from this group's members, some of whom noted, they felt like they "were being watched throughout by the staff," and the staff were generally "very unfriendly toward them" (QR 106, R 2.6 and TR 7 group interview 3 December 2007: 3).

Later on in the evening after the November session, while I was reflecting further on the Jew-Jewry conflict, I recalled another, *somewhat* similar, conflict with a staff member over too animated behavior in the underground sections. I then consulted my field notes for that day.

This had been with a group of grade eleven history students from a part of Berlin that was once in the former West, but that could be described as lower–middle class, so roughly equivalent in "class" status to their counterparts of East German background who had experienced the conflicts just explored.

Once we are all ready, we hand in our tickets and descend the staircase. A pupil, the class representative, a polite young woman who exuded confidence took the leading role and led the group immediately and very quickly out of the underground section directly to the permanent exhibition upstairs! They all followed her as she sped directly through the axes, without pausing to look at anything! I asked her about this once we were all at the top of the steps. What made you decide to come here first? Oh, I've been here before and know that this is where we are supposed to begin. This is the start. I find this absolutely remarkable. She, and all the group, actually ignored the underground section and began upstairs!

The visit is conducted with interest and some playfulness in the upper floors. Toward the end of the visit, they find their way to the Kadishman installation: upon entering this section, the mood is relaxed but more somber than before. Speech is quiet. Body language again more timid. One of the young men runs wildly over the installation. At this, a number of his classmates shake their heads and roll their eyes. The noise is impressive. Clanging echoes throughout. He then jumps and again—a loud clang. There is something approaching glee in his expression. Three of the young women walk over it, more controlled, slowly. Their expressions are hard to read but not smiling or frowning. Rather it is something in between. To me it looks like a sort of controlled seriousness. From here, they proceed directly downstairs to the underground axes. At first there is no talking, and the mood seems heavier. The body posture is also more rigid. A few read the signage on the walls, and they proceed to the Axis of the Holocaust. I also sense that they are getting restless. A group of the young women wait in front of the Holocaust Tower. There is no attendant there. They turn to me as I arrive and ask me if they are allowed to go inside. They seem a bit intimidated by the big door and hesitate to just go in, so I open it for them. The young women are silent in the tower, look up, walk around, one to the narrow corner at one end. The mood is heavy. They leave after less than a minute.

Then another part of the group enters, among them one of the young men, the same one who had run with glee over the Kadishman installation. He makes a clipped noise once he is inside the tower and it echoes. He seems pleased with the effect. At this point, an attendant (who must have shown up in the time I was inside) scolds him, "It is a memorial space not a playground!" The attendant, a young woman, is visibly angry, and she does not mask her con-

tempt for his behavior. She also looks kind of apologetically at me. Perhaps she did not know we were together? The young man stops right away and smiles sheepishly at me (Field diary from 2 July 2007).

There are many differences between this group and the one who experienced the Jew-Jewry conflict. This present group had been to the museum several times and had a fair amount of background on the topic (also from outside of school). Further, the young man who was scolded seemed to know his behavior was out of place: his sheepish grin, the reactions from his classmates, their rolling their eyes as he ran over the Kadishman masks, attest to this. He seemed then to be deliberately singing off tune (to borrow from Winter again). While, I am convinced that the young women of the Jew-Jewry episode were not intending to provoke at all. They asked me more than once throughout the visit what they had done wrong. The young man of this visit did not ask, and I believe he knew perfectly well why he had been scolded. Furthermore, for the other members of his visiting group, it was very much a memorial occasion. They, like he, knew he was being provocative in deliberately having fun as opposed to showing *Betroffenheit*. His classmates did display appropriate levels of dismay during the visit and expressed such feelings in their questionnaire replies. What both groups had in common, however, is that they were read by respective staff members as pupils behaving inappropriately.[3] That one was deliberately doing so, while the enthusiastic twins inadvertently gave offense, only became visible after the fact and in subsequent conversations.

Such specific expectations of how these young visitors should behave are thrown into sharp relief when one compares the experiences outlined above with how other tourists are received in the museum.

After-Reflections on Tourists— ("The Yanks Are Not Our Problem")

I continue to think about this Jew-Jewry episode, and the scolding of the echoing young man. In many previous and subsequent visits, I have observed visitors behaving a bit wildly here, most of them though were tourists from outside of Germany. I remember, for example, a school group from England, the accent I would judge as being "midland," and the age I would guess at about sixteen, were also loud in the axes and even in the tower. There was no scolding of them by the attendant. (It was, however, a different attendant.)

This group of pupils from England also had a tour, and I followed them for some time. I recall how the guide tried to engage them in discussion in the Rafael Roth Learning Center. She spoke in very good English with only a slight

German accent: "This museum is built around the concept of voids. That is emptiness. Something is missing. What do you think this symbolizes?"

She asks. No replies from the group. (That is no raised hands.) They just stare at her blankly. She tries again: "What is missing *here in Germany now? What is no longer here?" Aha finally, one young man puts his hand up, the guide nods to him. He replies quite seriously, "There are no more concentration camps." Here I do not read any joking or intended offense. The guide sighs, I see the exasperated look on her face. But she says only in a polite but slightly clipped tone, "The Jews are missing, and this architecture here by Daniel Libeskind symbolizes this."*

I decide to remain in the underground axes a bit longer. Eventually I see some teenagers with American accents running and laughing. I observe the staff: one, the visitor services representative who had tried to catch people to make them go upstairs first, notices them but just smiles at them. The attendant at the Holocaust Tower—one I remember who had been cross with some of my visitors who behaved in this way—does not approach them. Since I remember her, I approach her and mention in German that when I was here with a slightly unruly group of young visitors from a Berlin high school, she had scolded them. Why not now with these visitors? She clearly did not like my question and tensed up, but eventually replied, "What am I supposed to do? The Yanks are not our problem!"[4] I think she took my question to be an accusation that she was not doing enough to keep the visitors in line. Or perhaps she thought they were my problem? (Field diary 15 May 2008).

In comparing these interactions, it seems to me that it gave offense when those perceived as "Germans" behaved as tourists on this stage full of other tourists, but not when those perceived as Americans or British pupils got things "wrong" or behaved this way. In other words, Germans are the ones who are expected to perform a certain type of moved Germanness in this space.

My reading of these contrasting expectations is that the museum seems to be a rather dynamic stage, where different performances are expected or deemed appropriate depending on how the visitors in question are perceived or categorized. It may be fine for visitors thought to be English or American to behave as tourists, but it seems to offend when those perceived as German do this. Here again the persistence of the national as a key category of belonging, and thereby not belonging, is visible. The *Yanks* are not the concern of the staff member whom I spoke to. They are not *in the group* for which she feels responsible, whose performance might reflect on her.

I had mentioned that the large November visiting group, from the lower-class area of the former East, had been split into first-time and repeat visitors. Here the repeat visitors (not unlike the young women who avoided the underground sections of the museum introduced in Chapter 3) sought out the fun, multimedia aspects of the museum.

Clearly Expressed Boredom Punctuated by Interactives

Once I have given them their tickets and they have checked their coats and bags, they walk quickly and deliberately through the axes. It is a group of mostly young men (eleven out of the fifteen). They are quiet, and the body language is very relaxed. They chat with each other but again quietly. The entire group goes directly to the Garden of Exile, but they do not go out. I find this strange, since the weather is nice—a bit cold but dry—so as I see them walking back toward me, I ask why they didn't go out. "It is closed," says one of the young men. Oh, that's odd, I say and I go to check into it. I go and open the door. It is heavy and opens inward. The young men had tried to open it outward by pushing, and when this didn't work, they assumed it must be closed. The group seems thankful, the one a bit embarrassed. I mention that the door can be confusing, and they are not the first group to think they could not go out there. They walk among the pillars outside deliberately not playful. One young woman exclaims "My God!" She is visibly getting a bit dizzy and has to balance herself on a pillar. They only spend a short time here and come back in. It is indeed a bit cold without a jacket.

After this, part of the group proceeds to the Holocaust Tower; the rest looked at the displays along the walls in the axes. Inside the tower, a young man talked in a quiet tone and commented: "like at night" or "like in a concentration camp, really strange, cold." They do not spend much time and leave of their own accord.

This group skip the Rafael Roth Learning Center altogether. They proceed then up the steps to the permanent exhibition. In the "beginning" section, they remain quiet. Some add to the Wish Tree (the women first). Three young men take a moment to watch some kids having their photos taken by the tree. Two use the headphone display here at the beginning. This group spreads out more and is less enthusiastic than the first-time visitors from their class had been. One yawns—he was late—and looks both tired and bored. They then don't really engage with anything in this section on the Middle Ages.

A number of the group do stop in the next section. Some to use the Glikl wheel, others to play the Glikl packing game. This occupies them for a few minutes. They also crawl in the crawl space in the next section and one tries the backpack. Some from this group go to the headphone and listen to infor-mation about horse trading [see Figure 3.7]. In the next section on family life, the second group does pretty much the same thing as the first, but much quieter and with much less enthusiasm. They draw at the children's table and look through the viewer. They also go to and sit and listen at a nearby table, but do not bother to pick up any of the headphones, and the tired ones sit for a while on the blue round couch in the Heinrich Heine section. There is very little interaction with me, and they don't even pretend to be engaged. In the next section, two young women laugh quietly as they listen on headphones. Otherwise, there is almost no talking from this group. Then the young women handle drawers and laugh and comment on the old-fashioned hair dryer and iron. One exclaims "funny!" Others go to the cartoon booth, sit there and watch it for a while. The group is now moving faster through the museum.

After the Nazi era section, which they look over cursorily, the body language is what I would describe as tired, a bit slouched but not the same timidity or reserve of previous groups. One young man asks if there was anything else to see. I mention the section about Jews in Germany today, but the group indicated they were not at all interested in this. I asked then if they had seen the Kadish-man installation on past visits. No they had not. So I lead them there. They were quiet and just followed me. They looked at the installation for a while. Then two young men go and read the sign, which invites the visitors to walk over it. Then they walked over it without any obvious discomfort or emotion. Just sort of matter-of-factly. At this point, it was time to go, and the group was looking tired and bored. So we made our way to the meeting point, and they filled in the post-visit questionnaires quickly and individually. I thanked them and said I would see them again in a few days in class for the group discussion (Field diary 27 November 27).

What struck me the most at the time about most of the visitors in this group was that they did not make any effort to conceal clear boredom or affect interest. They were entertained on and off by some of the interactive possibilities, but generally were content just to kill the time there. There was hardly any enthusiasm evident (unlike the excited first-time visitors from their class). I recall too the groans coming from the young men at the back of the classroom when I had first mentioned the plan. I was left wondering why they had come. Was school even more boring perhaps? They could have done something else at school that day. Perhaps the museum was indeed a welcome distraction.

As I mentioned, I consulted the questionnaire replies from this class later that day. In addition to the indication of having no feelings on this topic that most of them attested, there was another reply type that I found quite curious, coming from a few of the young men who were repeat visitors. Namely, the equation of having feelings about the topic with either being religious or being Jewish. Here are three examples. (Recall that question 1.11 asks, Which feelings do you personally associate with Jewish history in Germany?) One young man wrote: "Jewry is a persuasion, I do not share this, but I accept other opinions" (QR 116, R 1.11). And in his answer to item 2.8 (Have your feelings about Jewish history in Germany changed after the museum visit?), he wrote: "No, I am still neutral with regards to the Jewish persuasion." Another replied to item 2.5 (What does it mean to you personally that this museum is in Berlin?) with, "This museum has no importance for me, but I think it is good for others that this museum is here, since they might themselves live with the Jewish religion" (QR 117). Two other classmates also gave similar indications, attesting "No [feelings] at all, since Jewry is not practiced in my family and the religion does not resonate with us. Religion basically does not matter to me, not only Jewry, but also all the others" (QR 112, R 1.11) and "no feelings, because of no particular interest in religion" (QR 111, R 1.11). I found these replies quite remarkable for a number of reasons. First, the equation with having to be religious, or Jewish even, in order to have feelings on the topic stood in sharp contrast to many of the respondents from previous groups who quite adamantly expressed strong feelings on this topic based on their Germanness, rather than religious affiliation, or lack thereof.

Further, the assumption visible here is that Jewish is an exclusively religious category, and I was struck again by this in light of the questions from the young women in the earlier visit that day, who had asked me why the Jews had not converted to escape persecution. It might also be, and here I do have to speculate again, that these adamant statements of nonreligiosity and lack of personal interest in the topic act too as a sort of protest against the West German dominant discourse. Here I am thinking with Goffman again, especially when he suggests that acts not in keeping with general expectations in an occasion may point to "an alienation from the social establishment or the institution" (Goffman 1963: 223). He also adds a "proviso not to over-emphasize the role of conscious thought and planning" (Goffman 1963: 173). Statements by the young men stressing no feelings about the topic because they themselves are not Jewish may well be such instances of expressed alienation. I return to this concept of alienation again in the next chapter.

Counterintuitive Results—The Meaning of the Word "Interest"

In going through the material from these visits and comparing it with other visiting groups in my study, I experienced initial confusion over seemingly contradictory questionnaire replies about their level of interest in German-Jewish history. In previous visits, many of the respondents of West German background attested a very high level of interest in the topic, while showing at some point clear signs of boredom in the museum. The opposite obtained with the first-time visitors from the group from the lower-class area of the former East. They ranked their level of interest as relatively low 2–3, but actually showed high levels of engagement in the museum. Upon further exploration with both groups, it became clear that they defined "interest" differently. I had asked a young man, of middle-class West German background, in a previous post-visit interview, who had ranked his interest as "5+" very high, but appeared quite bored in the museum, about this seeming discrepancy. He replied he had indicated such a high interest as for him it meant "a duty to be engaged with this topic," not how much he liked it or not. He even said he would recommend the museum further as he feels a *gewisser Zwang* (a certain compulsion) to go there and address the topic (Field diary 2 July 2007), even though he also indicated it did not contain anything new for him. When I asked members of these first-time visitors about their low indications of interest in the topic, despite their having enjoyed the visit, replies were as follows: "I am more interested in ancient Rome and Greece. So I was not really interested in Jewish history" and "I am more interested in the religious conflicts between Muslims and Christians" and "I find Egyptian history more interesting" (TR 7 focus group interview of 3 December 2007: 2). From these replies, it seems that they did not qualify the word interest in the same way that their counterpart of West German background had. For them, interest meant something along the lines of "curiosity about" and was not connected with duty or a sense of compulsion.

This understanding that the word interest was defined differently helps to shed light on the seemingly contradictory material. Clearly, if interest is meant as duty then it does not contradict actually being bored with the topic or the museum. And indicating a low interest may not at all mean that visitors will lack engagement with the topic and the museum, especially if they have not yet been oversaturated with it, or had otherwise miseducative experiences (in Dewey's sense) with it. Problems in interpretation and understanding occur when one universally assumes common meanings to common words. Moreover, this episode, I think, acts then as a reminder to delve deeper in social research to avoid superficial readings of what are in fact rather complex situations.

In terms of theory on "memory" and its relevance to these situations, I am reminded again of the appropriateness of Jay Winter's metaphor mentioned earlier of remembrance as a sing-along. In a sing-along or a choir, it can become very noticeable and disturbing to those expecting a choral performance when some sing off-tune, sing the wrong song, or fail to sing at all. Further, at times, singers may be aware of this and be deliberately singing off key. While, at other times, this is not intentional, and they may be unaware of the expectation that they sing in a certain way, might not have learned the words or the tune, for example, or might not have had much choir practice in preparation. Finally, certain visitors are indeed expected to sing certain songs. Staying with this metaphor for the moment, let us turn our attention to another group of choral singers, who indeed sang another tune. Moreover, they were not expected to perform *Betroffenheit* as such, since they were hardly recognized as belonging to the German national collective.

Notes

1. Note that at the time this text was written, using the masculine form as a universal was an unquestioned norm.
2. At the time, I hesitated to go into more detail since, while I was confident enough to touch on Judaism and Christianity. I had not yet read the Koran and was not particularly familiar with the tenets and practices of Islam. These young visitors would likely have benefited from a JMB tour that highlights the parallels between Judaism and Islam, provided that it offered enough background information.
3. Irit Dekel has come across similar conflicts in her work at the Holocaust Memorial. In her research, unlike in mine, the assumed origin of the visitors was mentioned directly by staff: "Guides and hosts occasionally say that 'some visitors from the East do not know where they are and hence behave in a disrespectful manner'" (Dekel 2009: 77).
4. Die Amis sind nicht unser Problem!

Chapter 5

Between Engagement, Playful Appropriation, and Exclusion

The Visit as a Fun Day Out with the Class

In order to put this visit into context, I would like to introduce you to the pupils and teacher as I first met them. Further, I describe the visit in some depth so as to convey the general mood and atmosphere of the day. This is a *Gymnasium* in a part of Berlin with a majority population of Turkish background. It is just north of my home and is, in fact, administratively in the same district. This was also one of the few schools, whose history department head replied quickly and directly to my letter request for a group to visit the JMB. He called me within the week and praised the JMB and the very positive experiences he had had there with his pupils. He has recommended a grade eleven history class, and I arrange to visit it the following week.

An Interested and Energetic Class

It is a busy fall morning. There is a lot of traffic on the way to the school as it is rush hour. Luckily, it is only a couple kilometers away. The school itself would not be easy to find if one did not know it was there. It is behind a high wall in a rather crowded part of the city. I have to ring from outside this wall to be let in. I wait in the office to be collected by Mr. R., as had been arranged. He comes very soon. He makes an immediate good impression on me: very easy going, pleasant, a bit older than myself. It is just before school starting time (8:00 a.m.), and some pupils are still arriving. As I enter the hallway, I notice that the school is badly in need of a paint job. The building seems very run down. Walking through the school, young men, senior pupils, open the doors for the teacher and myself on several occasions. This gesture always catches me off guard. I still cannot get used to people opening doors for me or for teachers. I cannot remember this ever happening in my high school in Canada!

We enter the classroom. The pupils seem to be in a good mood. The high energy level in the room is palpable. The pupils chat with one another. Mr R. soon asks the group to be quiet and then I introduce myself and the project. They all listen and do not interrupt. They also seem to understand me well and do not giggle at my accent or mistakes in German. (This had disturbed me in a previous school visit.) One young woman asks if she can also take part even though she knows the museum well and had recently done an internship there. I say, of course, no problem. She seems happy about this, as does most of the class about the visit in general. I did not perceive any rolled eyes or groans. The group expresses enthusiasm about the upcoming visit as well as a lot of curiosity about me personally, asking me about Canada and how I ended up in Berlin. One young woman also asks if she can practice her English with me. So we chat a bit. Her English is very good, and I mention this. "Oh, we are from Pakistan and speak a lot of English," she retorts. I chat a little more with Mr R., and he says he really likes his pupils. They are very charming, he says. Indeed, they seem very likeable, and many have expressed a keen interest in the topic and the museum. They also seem to like and respect their teacher. They had listened to him right away, when he told them to be quiet before I introduced myself, for example. Mr R. mentions that he does not plan to prepare them specifically for the visit. He is curious and a bit apprehensive about how it will be. He will be there for the visit to keep an eye on things. We part ways, having arranged the time and day for the visit. I am very much looking forward to the museum visit next month with this friendly group (Field diary 28 September 2007).

A Fun Day Out!

The pupils arrive at the museum on time. Mr R. was there early. I explain the security procedure to them; some are familiar with it already. They are clearly excited and cheerful and are a bit loud and boisterous. The teacher says he will be around now and then in the museum, but will not follow the group the entire time.

They are very energetic, especially the young men. As soon as we are through security and have given the tickets in, the large group (twenty-four in all) proceeds down the stairs. Then they split up into somewhat smaller groups along gender lines. The young men shove each other, joke, and laugh. Three young women have broken off to the side and look at a display behind glass embedded in the wall. It is an open but neatly packed child's suitcase. They talk quietly about it with one another. Another small group of young women listens intently for a while to a nearby guide who is talking about the Libeskind design in English.

The groups spend some time here in the axes. Then some proceed toward the Holocaust Tower. Here, a large group, this time comprised of both young men and women enter with me. It is cold today. They huddle a bit together. They do speak, but in a hushed tone. They all look up. We exit soon. An attendant opens the door to let more pupils from the class in as I leave with this first group.

Generally, in the axes the young men, especially, are noisy. They go outside to the Garden of Exile without looking at any of the artifacts or reading anything along the way. Then they start to run among the columns. They are playing tag! And hiding behind the columns every now and again. At this, one of the young men from the class comes up to me and apologizes on behalf of his classmates, saying that they don't know how to behave here. He appears quite embarrassed. He is blushing. He is one of the two young men who claimed German back-ground in the class.[1] I reply to him that he need not apologize to me, that I am not bothered by the game. Some time later, I see that he and the classmate he spent most time with, the other young man of German background, have joined enthusiastically in the game of tag/hide and seek. The two young men jump more than once from the wall, where groups often sit or lean, to the ground in front of the columns. I wonder if this might be dangerous since the ground is not level, but see that no one is hurting themselves. I am also watch-ing other visitors, who look for a moment at them but say and do nothing, and also see a member of staff, an older woman, who actually steers clear of this group, which surprised me as I had expected that they would get scolded for their wild behavior.

This sort of running and playing hide and seek is something I have seen oc-casionally at the Holocaust Memorial, but this is the first time I have seen this here at the JMB. Later two young women also join the game. Coming back in after the game of tag one young man makes a Jewish joke losing his balance say-ing "Hey look, now I'm a Jew." I hear this as does the blushing classmate who had previously apologized to me, and he goes even a deeper shade of red, while smiling at me. This is truly unlike any other visit I have accompanied. I won-der how the staff will react to this. So far, the staff have not intervened at all. On the occasions when I notice staff members noticing us, they appear nervous and timid. I decide I am going to follow some of the more energetic young men closely to see how the visit progresses. They are having fun and so am I actually, but I do wonder if other visitors are offended by this very animated behavior.[2]

The Rafael Roth Learning Center is closed today (for filming), and so the groups do not go in. They proceed directly upstairs after the game of tag, joking and pushing each other as they climb the stairs. They are loud, and at some point on the way up seem to notice this and they hush each other. One young woman looks quietly at a display, while others go to the Wish Tree and add to it. The group is quieter here. This is the reverse of many of the other visits I have observed where the quietness in the underground sections contrasts to louder speech upstairs. The group divides as follows: the young men form one big group of about twelve, while the young women form smaller groups and occasionally go off alone.

The young men speed through the next sections and only stop briefly to try to fit into a tunnel. Three young women do stop and go to the interactive video game—the one about packing for a trading trip. I am following the group of twelve young men at this point so leave the young women behind. They keep going until they get to the Moses Mendelssohn coin machine. This gets their attention, and they try to use the machine. I intervene to say it only takes five-cent pieces, that using anything else might not work. I have a few of these and hand them out. The young men spend some time here. The mood is jovial. The body language is very relaxed, and they become loud again. I notice a member of staff, a young woman, looking at the group with a worried expression. I catch her eye, and she smiles at me. I go up to her and ask if anything is wrong? No, she says, the boys are just a bit loud, maybe you could ask them to be quieter? she asks. I say of course, but do wonder why she did not approach them, or me, directly.

In the next section about family life, two young women go to the small table and draw pictures, while three young men go to the viewer and fight over it. "Hey man, it's my turn!" One of the groups of young women have caught up to us and now take a moment to look at the wall displays. Later young men push each other to get seats at the table about the emancipation of the Jews. Often enough, the two young men who had emphasized their German background are much quieter than their classmates and seem to notice my presence and give me sideways glances and apologetic looks. They are also quite friendly and chat to me now and again throughout the visit. The young women from this group are not at all loud now and smile often at me.

A bit later, many go to a cartoon booth, which shows an animated film called Alice and the Fire Department. Here, both women and men cram into the narrow booth, relax, chat, recline, and sit. Some could not fit in and so go off to other sections. The speech gets louder again and more animated inside the booth. One young man asks: "It's cool, but what's Jewish about it?" After a few minutes, I leave them in the booth and go on to check on the few others from the class who are elsewhere. I find some young women in the next section, and one asks about the metal discs she can see through the window. She asks if I can tell her how to get there. Her classmate intervenes saying she knows where it is and can take her to them. The two young men of German background stick together throughout the visit and speed through the section on the First World War and the Weimar Republic. They do stop at the children's world section and play there for a bit along with two young women who also found this. They climb up the ramp and draw something too.

The cartoon booth group finally emerges and speed through these sections. In the section on persecution under the Nazis, they do not look at anything at all; one says, "It's boring. I don't feel like it anymore." Two young women give quick glances to the displays on the walls about deportation and extermination. The others skip it altogether. The two young men of German background do watch a short video about the Auschwitz trial and listen to some information on headphones about this. Now a large group of young men say they are done, and one asks if they can leave. I say "sure" and mention that I am going to the place with the metal masks to find the young women who had wanted to see it just to make sure they found it okay. "Oh, we would like to see that too!," they say. So, I bring this large group of men (I count ten now) with me to the Kadishman display.

The young women from before are indeed there, but they are not walking on the installation. One of the young men walks quickly to the other side and back, another loses his balance and needs to lean on another. They did not read the sign, inviting them to walk on the masks, before walking over them. The mood is still jovial, but they are no longer loud. They even seem a bit tired. There is much less physicality. Now they want to leave, so I direct them out. We do have to walk through the underground axes again in order to get to the exit. Being down here seems to excite them again. One young man, dressed all in white sport clothing, takes out a music player and plays some Turkish music, which is audible to everyone but not loud. He struts quickly through the axes and up the steps. We all regroup now at the meeting point. Mr R. is waiting for us. He asks how it went. I said it was interesting, and they seemed to have fun, especially playing tag in the Garden of Exile. Mr R. rolls his eyes. "That's silly," he comments. The group gathers quickly. I hand out the post-visit questionnaires, and they fill them out. After several minutes, they are done. We all have to exit together this time since this group had entered via the back and put their coats and bags in one large coat-check box.

Once out front of the museum again, I turn to the group who are still gathered together. Mr R. stays with them too saying he wants to be sure to escort them back to school. I thank them for taking part and say I will be in the classroom on Friday to talk about the visit. I end with the words, "You're free to go." At this, a group of young women starts signing: "Einigkeit und Recht und Freiheit." (The opening lines of the German national anthem, literally: "unity, and law, and freedom."³) At this, Mr R. intervenes, stern but friendly: "No, no, that's enough, not here. Don't be so silly!" They stop singing, and we all cross the street together. I proceed to my bike, while the group and Mr R. go in the direction of the nearby subway (Field diary 24 October 2007).

Between Participation, Confusion, and Exclusion

After this fun and remarkable visit, I was eager to read their questionnaire replies. Many of the replies were not particularly surprising to me given my impressions of the pupils. There were repeated references to the game of tag in the Garden of Exile, for example. The majority of the participants also expressed a keen interest in the topic. One of the young men of Turkish background specifically noted that he wanted "to know a lot about Jewry" and that to date most of his knowledge on the topic has come from "history class, books, television, home" (QR 60, R 1.9, 1.10). A young woman, who described herself as "Turkish actually Kurdish" and Muslim, noted that she knew about the topic from "history books, in class, television, novels" and feels "sad about the pogroms, amazed that such a culture has existed for thousands of years" (QR 53, R 1.10, 1.11).

Yet another young woman, who described herself as Turkish-Kurdish and Muslim, wrote of her engagement with the topic and the museum at some length:

> I heard about Jewish history from my older sister when she covered the topic of National Socialism at school. I was 11 or 12 then. I have seen a lot on television, such as documentaries and movies like "Schindler's List." I have read a lot in school and also outside of school on the topic of "Jewish history," like "experiences in concentration camps" or "Anne Frank." Since I have read and heard a lot, I associate oppression and terror etc. with the topic. (QR 73, R 1.10, 1.11)

She went on to relate her impressions of the museum as follows:

> Well, since I was pretty well informed beforehand, I didn't really learn more. I only got some information about Jews in the Middle Ages, I already knew about everything else … sometimes I did not know what the architects wanted to express with their art … It was very cold in the Holocaust Tower and I guess this was supposed to demonstrate how it might have been back then. The works of art are depressing and one had the urge to get away and look for a way out (QR 73, R 2.1–2.4). [She had one critique as follows]: I did not like it that one tried to present the Holocaust through works of art, since I am of the opinion that this is not possible. [But, generally enjoyed the visit noting]: my respect for Jewish history has increased. I feel a bit close to them since my people are also oppressed. (QR 73, R 2.8)

Her replies are an illustration of how one may find a way to relate to this topic without the need for "guilt," or Germanness as such. Key again is previous knowledge of and a cultivation of a personal connection to the topic, which can take many forms and need not necessarily, only be that of the dominant discourse of *Betroffenheit*. Michael Rothberg and Yasemin Yildiz recognize that archives of migrant memory, as a sort of multidirectional memory, which moves beyond ethnically based concepts of German memory as such, do exist (Rothberg and Yildiz 2011: 37). The question I would ask is how these possibilities are experienced by their practitioners and perceived in practice in and by the surrounding society. Are they viewed, for example, as equal to, or as valid as the dominant discourse, which is still very much in the hands of elites of West German background? Irit Dekel in her empirical work has found that: "Jews, as well as other Holocaust victim groups and migrant groups in Germany today, are not equal subjects of memory, meaning both that their subjectivity as participants in the public sphere is limited to specific roles, times and spaces, and that inter-subjective communication about their representation is limited" (Dekel 2016: 1).

I would like to take a moment to explore one aspect of Rothberg and Yildiz's findings. The authors describe a publicly funded initiative called the *Stadtteilmutter* (neighborhood mothers) project. This began as a social welfare project and included employing women of migrant background, many of them of Turkish background and Muslim religion. Their job was to reach out to the members of their own community and to provide such welfare there. The authors note that "by virtue of their linguistic and cultural knowledge, the mothers would be able to address segments of the population beyond the reach of majority German welfare workers" (Rothberg and Yildiz 2011: 39). Later these women actively sought to create their own projects, which engaged with history and politics including the Nazi past from their own perspectives. The authors go on to praise this project noting that the participation of the woman amounted to making them "activist citizens" (Rothberg and Yildiz 2011: 40).

While I do share Rothberg and Yildiz's commitment to taking the memorial archives of Germans of non-German background seriously and recognizing the entanglements present therein, I do hesitate to fully apply such concepts to the German situation. I recall a colleague of mine, a fellow anthropologist who had helped to run the *Stadtteilmutter* project, recounted the following: she was fond of the project and also produced a photograph of the Mayor of *Neukölln*, Heinz Buschkowsky, with a large number of smiling women wearing head scarves surrounding him. "How happy they look," I remarked. My colleague agreed noting that they do get a lot out of this work, but sometimes there are problems. One of the women took her *Stadtteilmutter* job confirmation to the immigration authority (in German this is called the *Ausländerbehörde* containing the word foreigner in it) in order to get her residence permit renewed. The official there just scoffed at it, saying it is merely an "employment measure" (*Beschäftigungsmaßnahme)* and not a real job. My colleague noted that there was not much she could do to cheer this devastated woman up. She was very upset, because she will have to leave the country soon. (This conversation took place during a colloquium at my institute in May 2007.)

I think one has to be aware that many legal migrants still do not have citizenship rights (even after decades of working here and paying taxes). Crucially, the power asymmetry between the *Ausländerbehörde* and these women needs to be taken into consideration in order to put such projects into context. The gulf will take more than cultural participation (even though this too has value) to fill. I worry, too, that Mr Buschkowsky might just content himself with this photo-op and the moral capital he might be able to gain from it, so as appear to support integrative processes, and stop at this sort of cultural endeavor rather than tackle the, in my view more pressing, need for political and legal participatory rights. As happy as being a *Stadtteilmutter* may have made her feel, the risk of being expelled trumps that.

Let us return now to the young museum visitors. Two of the features of the questionnaire replies surprised me and stood out immediately: first, several references to the "concentration camp" (*KZ* or *Konzentrationslager*) part of the museum, and second, repeated comments that the staff was unfriendly. I recall that I found the staff to be timid and was surprised, as I did not see them intervene during the visit. In the group interview, I bring up the points that I found most intriguing on the questionnaire replies:

> To my question regarding what you might most remember, many of you wrote "KZ." Did you mean the Holocaust Tower?
>
> (A general nodding and several say): Yes.
>
> And how did you connect this with a concentration camp?, I ask.
>
> One of the young women who I had seen entering the tower as I left replies:
>
> We went in there and it was really, very cold—one could feel the cold from far away—and I when the woman closed the door got scared.
>
> (Her classmate adds): And one could not get out. So, the walls were very high. There was no way out. (TR 5 group interview 29 October 2007: 2)

Another had noted her impressions of the tower as follows: "It was, in my view, frightening in the Holocaust Tower. The darkness, this thin sliver of light, and then this dependence on another person. That one has to wait until someone from the staff opens the door again from the outside" (QR

68, R 2.3). Here too then, as in previous situations I have described, the visitors thought they had to wait to be let out of the tower. Unlike most of the previous visitors, however, this led many in this group to conclude that this structure was meant to be a concentration camp–like space.

It was only in thinking about these two situations after the fact and remembering that the attendant had indeed left for a moment after these young woman had entered that I realized that they must have spent quite some time "trapped" in the tower. I was not in the tower with them as I had been with the previous group. I also then recalled the repeated comments I overheard like, "Let's go in the gas chamber!" Considering this situation and the fact that these respondents had not yet been to an actual concentration camp memorial, this "confusion" starts to make some sense. One could also speculate on other possible influences such as the media presence of images and terms related to the camps, as did staff members when I asked them subsequently about the prevalence of visitors perceiving this structure as a concentration camp or gas chamber. On more than one occasion in my interviews with staff members, they confirmed that this is not a too unusual occurrence.[4] Another contributing factor might also be that such confusion does indeed arise from the expectation of authenticity that is often a part of the social practice of museum visiting. That the JMB does indeed call itself a museum and not a memorial, might also be part of the reason why this issue of expecting, and in some cases thinking that one has seen, an actual reproduction of a gas chamber, for example, is as prevalent as it seems to be.

It was, in fact, an episode sparked by this confusion that led to a conflict with a member of museum staff, which I did not see myself. It was later recounted to me during the group interview:

> When we wanted to go into the tower there was a woman there and we were thinking out loud, "What could this be?" And the woman yelled at us right away, "No it is nothing like that!" She also did not tell us what it was. She only said, "It is nothing at all like what you think." Then she let us in. And then she opened the door and yelled inside: "Be quiet please!" She was really in a bad mood. (TR 5 of group interview from 29 October 2007: 4)

This young woman was one of the visitors who did indeed "mistake" the tower for a "KZ" (concentration camp). What I found surprising here is that the attendant did not bother to explain a more abstract possible meaning to the room. She just told them they were wrong and to be quiet. She cut them out of any possible conversation on the topic. I do have to admit that I was alarmed that she would disregard their questions as I recalled the many times I had been in the museum with family and friends and always had any questions I had very courteously and quite thoroughly addressed. After all, is not asking questions a sign of interest in the topic? Or is only "dismayed" interest worthy of consideration? Does the general boisterous behavior of the group, and how they are perceived, render that interest null and void—or at least not worthy of being taken seriously? Are they too excluded from the group of concern as the "Yanks" had been?

Between Resignation and Actively Seeking Inclusion: "We Are Just a Neukölln Group"—"It Was a Neukölln Class, After All"

Another reply to my question about the unfriendly staff coming from one of the young men was to sit back in his chair, open his arms wide, and shrug and say, "We are just a Neukölln Group" (TR 5 group interview 29 October 2007: 5). (Neukölln is the region of the city where they reside and is often portrayed as a troubled area or social hot spot.) He seemed to take the contempt of the staff in his stride as something to be expected and not particularly remarkable. This "halt" (in the German original), "just" in my translation, and wide-armed shrug gesture suggests to me that this is something quite normal for him. Much later in reply to a follow-up question to Mr R. about how he himself perceived the visit, and the aside that he had been the only teacher during this study that actually attended the visit throughout with his pupils, Mr R. commented emphatically, "Of course I came with! It was a Neukölln class, after all! There were a lot of Muslims." He continued, adding, "the visit was exciting. I was not disappointed. There was neither anything negative nor anything surprisingly positive—no extreme situations." He had also indicated that the Jewish museum "tends to be pupil-friendly. It adapts to their wishes" (Interview 12 December 2010). The teacher's use of the word *schließlich* (after all) much like his pupil's "halt" suggests a tendency to expect a certain type of behavior and reception.

In probing this issue further, it is helpful to compare the perspectives on the visit. The teacher found no extreme situations, while the young women experienced the staff as very unfriendly, while I myself saw the staff as timid and standoffish. These differing interpretations of the same visit are very likely related to expectations and previous experiences. In my own reading of the day, I had been implicitly comparing this visit to those of other school groups, especially those who had been expected to be inside the dominant culture of *Betroffenheit*.

Mr R. had likely encountered more extreme situations with his classes, while a number of the young women found the staff particularly hostile.

Further, during the visit itself Mr R. had described their playing tag in the Garden of Exile and singing the German national anthem outside the museum as "silly," but not as offensive.[5] I too viewed the singing as a sort of playful appropriation of a national symbol, especially given that the singers did not self-identify as German. It is crucial here to understand these differing perspectives on the day not in terms of more true or more legitimate, but rather to see them as all relevant and, more importantly differently positioned perspectives. It is in my view crucial to recognize and value varying positionalities in order to open up discursive space and challenge problematic universals, be they small scale as in the views of the visit explored here, or larger scale in terms of "shared" memory and political belonging.

It is precisely this—the recognition of different positionalities as valid and worthy of inclusion—that is so crucial in order to question the exclusionary mechanisms like the ones explored above. Moreover, making the unmarked dominant discourse visible is also crucial. Rather than being a taken-for-granted norm, it is also partial and positioned. Issues of exclusion are, naturally, not limited to the JMB, but operate throughout the culture of memory. Damani Partridge in his research on Holocaust memory with young Berliners of Turkish and Arab background, referring to a general lack of interest in the topic,[6] asks, "To what extent was their absence linked to the failure of the perpetrator discourse to include them, with its emphasis on German guilt? [and found] … that the implicit demand for this affiliation with the guilt of historical perpetration was producing new specters of exclusion" (Partridge 2010: 821–22).

Viola Georgi (2003) in her research into how young people of "migrant background" relate to Germany's historical legacy also came across a troubling illustration of the problem. Here, I would like to relate it at length as reading it was a sort of epiphany for me and has helped to put my own material into a broader context: Georgi introduces us to Bülent (a pseudonym, of course), a young man of Turkish origin who went on a trip to the *Theresienstadt* concentration camp/ghetto memorial. Bülent was born in Germany as was his mother, and he has German citizenship. Yet he is still referred to as a migrant, and even calls himself a foreigner.[7] Bülent relates how the trip came about:

> So it was set up at school. I was, well, the only one from our class. The others were not actually interested in it … There was say 50 percent Germans in the class and I was the only foreigner, as it were, that was interested in it.[8] (Georgi 2003: 151)

He then proceeds to describe a conflict during the trip:

> At the site, many were crying and all. The girls were really upset by it. As for myself, I did not feel the need to cry … it is, naturally, sad. I mean I would not like to live that way. Anyway, and when I said: "Why are you crying, actually? You don't have to cry about it, think about it." Then there was once again this: "Hey, you foreigner, you really have no idea." [He then continues] And there was a point when I got annoyed, since I cannot accept it: (*gesticulating excitedly*). First: I was not allowed to come here. I was born here. Second: I have a German passport. Third: I speak the language perfectly … I don't feel like a foreigner here. Somehow, I am also German, but somehow also Turkish. I am both. (Georgi 2003: 152)[9]

I cannot help but draw some parallels between the museum visit with the students on this "fun day out" and Bülent's rather more disturbing encounter. And I do have to admit that I have myself come to experience disbelief and anger at such situations. I see them as examples of when remembering this history of the Nazi crimes acts as a mechanism of exclusion. Here Germans of German background play the more powerful role of excluders, and those of non-German background are quite literally left out of the conversation, even in those cases when they demonstrate a desire to find a way inside as Bülent had.

Let us revisit now the issue of positionality with the museum visitors from Neukölln. The young man's shrug and "We are just a Neukölln class," his teacher's use of "after all" in a very similar sentence, and here Bülent's "There it was once again" not only indicate a familiarity with the very particular treatment they came to expect, but also an awareness of their own positionality. Compare this with the universal statements by the young men of German background from the elite circles explored in Chapter 3: when they described "how things were done in Germany," and "the people, who behave in a calmer and more conscious way" in the museum. These were considered the norm, to be universally applicable (in Germany),[10] and were thus left unmarked. There seems to be a lack of awareness here, on the part of these future elites, of their own partiality in this setting.

Returning now to the young women who indicated that they were upset by their reception by the staff: one recounted the following: "No matter what we did, it was always as if we were being watched. And then they come and tell us off, instead of being friendly" (TR 5 group interview 29 October 2007: 5).

Pierre Bourdieu's contributions on the appropriation of space might be helpful in analyzing this situation:

> At the risk of feeling themselves out of place, individuals who move into a new space must fulfil the conditions that that space tacitly requires of its occupants. This may be the possession of a certain cultural capital [this can be anything from body mannerisms to pronunciation], the lack of which can prevent the real ap-

propriation of supposedly public goods … Museums come to mind." (Bourdieu 1999: 128)

Such a lack of "real" appropriation may well be at play here, not only because of their boisterous behavior, but also because of their group attribution as a *Neukölln* group and, therefore, as one actually not expected to perform as "Germans" or in other words not assumed to belong to the dominant culture.

This group dynamic and attribution is visible too in the case of another young woman who indicated that she was disturbed by the unfriendliness of the staff. She wrote that something unexpected that came up in her visit was that the staff had "become unfriendly" (QR 54, R 2.2). She had in the months preceding this group visit taken part in an internship at the JMB, which she said she very much enjoyed. She was quite equipped with the "cultural capital" necessary to appropriate this space. She was well informed about the museum and the topic. She noted her previous exposure to the subject as coming from her relatives, school, television, the internet, and the museum itself (QR 54, R 1.10). She attested a personal connection to the subject. And her feelings on the topic she expressed eloquently and empathetically as follows:

> It is very sad to learn about the history and the genocide. When one imagines oneself in the position of the people back then, then one is appalled about what happened to them. What the Jews had to experience and go through is horrible. Always being on the run and being afraid is terrible. It is a very dramatic history and for me personally also a very sad one. (QR 54, R 1.11)

Perhaps the cultural or even moral capital that might be read from her previous positioning is rendered invalid when one is perceived in certain situations and environments as part of a "*Neukölln* group."[11]

Let us also compare my own observations of their reception with those explored in Chapter 4. Those visitors were far less animated than this group had been, and yet they were scolded repeatedly. It seems that they were perceived as being in the group who were expected to perform *Betroffenheit* properly, while this group was not, even though, they too experienced disdain from staff members.

I must have looked a bit shocked at the description of the unfriendly attendant. (Remember I had found the staff to be rather timid in their interactions with this group, in fact they had to me seemed reluctant to even approach them.) In reaction to my bewildered facial expression, another young woman from this group went on to explain that after leaving the tower, two of them walked around the museum and found another staff member, who was much nicer and explained to them what the tower was. Interestingly, though, they were still left with the impression that it was a concentration camp reproduction as the following exchange from the group interview suggests:

> Later it was indeed what we had originally thought.
>
> [Her classmate adds] One of the staff members was actually very friendly. We kind of bombarded her [with questions] a little. Only the one was friendly. The others just watched us and gave us looks.
>
> [The first speaker then elaborates.] They didn't actually want to explain things to us when we had questions. They did not help us at all. They just walked around.
>
> [I ask]—Did you ask questions?—Yes [they reply in unison].
>
> [Another young woman adds.]
>
> By this guide, questions were addressed that the other staff, for example could not answer. When we came out the tower, I simply stood beside a guide and just listened. (TR 5 group interview 29 October 2007: 4)

What I also found noteworthy here, is the way these young women refused to accept, or resign themselves to, the dismissive attitude they experienced from the Holocaust Tower attendant. They found strategies to get the recognition they desired: walking around until they found a staff member who would help them and listening in on a tour in progress. I find it troubling that they had to go through many people before finding one ready to engage with them. What is also significant is that these two young women received the recognition—and some parity of participation—they sought only after they had broken off from the group—thus physically distancing themselves from it—in order to seek out answers to their questions. This dynamic appears to be the mirror image of what their classmate had experienced. She had been accepted in the JMB as an individual intern, but not as part of her school group.

Through Goffman's Lens—Alienation and Protest

Returning to the concept of occasioned behavior, it seems to me that this visit seemed to have much more to do with a fun day out than with either a memorial or a tourist occasion. Recall that Goffman's assertion that "the same physical space may be caught within the domain of different social occasions" (1963: 20). Further, he posits that provocative acts or "the failure to exhibit presence in an occasion" can be "an expression of alienation from and hostility to the gathering itself and the officials in it" (25) or "an alienation from the social establishment or the institution" (223). These ideas are worth contemplating although they do not necessarily apply to all the discrete episodes.

Some of the behavior of the young men can be read as a sort of provocation, and perhaps also as an expression of a deliberate oppositional reading of the space in Stuart Hall's terms, especially of the underground sections of the museum. I would consider the game of tag in the Garden of Exile and the Jewish jokes afterward in this light. Might not the young men be performing a sort of protest as in: we do not need to perform here. This is not our culture.

Consider the initial embarrassment of the young man of German background and his apologies to me. I would argue that they function performatively to separate him from the group who "did not know how to behave here." He may well have been willing to perform "correctly" had I demanded it of him. Indeed, he began with more timid and reserved behavior in these sections. It was a space he could claim as his in that he "knew how to behave," unlike his classmates. He actually looked first surprised and then pleased, when I told him I was not bothered by the game. Then he was more than happy to join in the game, as energetically, if not more so, than his classmates. Had I given him permission to break the unwritten rules? He was nevertheless embarrassed again, and apologetic to me, at the joke and accompanying gesture, "Look, I'm a Jew," by his classmate. (Were such jokes a step too far out of line for him? Was he worried that I would finally get offended?)

From Protest to Entanglement—From the JMB to Israel

Although the majority of the pupils from this class expressed interest in and personal connections to the topic, a few of the questionnaire replies also point to a sort of protest against and alienation from the topic as presented in the museum. One young man, who had described himself as Turkish and Muslim, wrote that the museum's location had for him had "no meaning. It could be in Bavaria. It's all the same to me." Further, his predominant feeling in the museum was, "boredom," and he then emphasized his impressions of the topic had not changed at all after this visit: "No, not at all. Since I knew everything that happened already, and most of it was of no great importance to me" (QR 52, R 2.5, 2.4, 2.7). One of his classmates, who described himself as Turkish, although he noted that his mother was German, also expressed a general feeling of "boredom" in the museum, and added that his feelings on the topic itself were, "Mixed feelings. During the films, sadness, sympathy. But when I see reports about the Gaza Strip on television." And in terms of engagement with specific sections of the museum, he noted that in the underground axes, Holocaust Tower, and Garden of Exile: "I actually didn't have any feelings in these spaces related to Jews." In reply to the question on his impressions in the upper floor sections: "Oh boy, there are some good looking girls here. But still sympathy killed with no sympathy!" (QR 65, R 2.1, 2.3, 2.4). I do get the impression that in this case, he was performing a sort of protest and expressing a deliberate oppositional reading of the space, which stand in contrast to the dominant discourse on the topic. He focused on a preoccupation with "good looking" girls in the museum, and noting that his sympathy for the victims of the Holocaust, while there, was "killed" by lack of sympathy for Israelis, for example.

Another one of his classmates gave similar replies. This young man indicated that he was Palestinian-Lebanese from Haifa-Palestine and Muslim. He indicated that he already knew "almost all of Jewish history," which he learned "in certain Arabic books, history class, the internet, television (from Arabic channels—series)." He wrote that he felt both "Sympathy [and] a bit of hatred." In terms of his feelings in the underground sections of the museum, he noted: "It was fun in the garden. It was fun to play tag there. In the tower, it was cold and dark, but I found it cool to stand in such a huge dark, cold room." Of the permanent exhibition, he stated: "To be honest, I found it mostly boring, except for certain parts." The JMB's location "had no meaning for him." And his feeling on the topic had not changed, "I still have sympathy for them because of the thing with Hitler. I only hold a grudge against Jews in Israel" (QR 55, R 1.9 to 2.8).

During the group interview, when I asked about indicated connections to Israel and the Gaza Strip, there was silence and uncomfortable glances. Nobody, it seemed, wanted to discuss these issues in the group setting. This was the case even though their teacher, Mr R., had excused himself for the duration of the interview. (He had asked if this was okay, as he wanted to meet with a student who had missed some classes to give her a chance to catch up.) I mention this here since other scholars have noted a habitus of carefulness on these topics, on the part of teachers. Karoline Georg and her colleagues describe the activities of a group called the Kreuzberg Initiative against Anti-Semitism (KIgA). They highlight the situation of teachers turning to KIgA for guidance in how to teach their students of Turkish and Arab backgrounds about conflicts in the Middle East. Many teachers do not feel equipped to deal with anti-Semitism. Further discussing the conflict in the Middle East is often formed by the view among teachers that they cannot openly deal with this problem since a free expression on this topic without a moral positioning is impossible. The resulting insecurity on the part of teachers regarding how to address this topic with their classrooms full of Muslim students is reflected in increased demand for educational modules from KIgA (Cf. Georg, Niehoff, and Demirel 2009: 228).

Thus, I am limited here in my analysis of this illustration to observations in the museum and the questionnaire replies. Nevertheless, I do find the replies noteworthy, especially the way this young man not only deliberately expressed an oppositional reading of the Holocaust Tower in that he "found it cool to be in such a huge, dark, cold room," but also separated the topic of the Jews who had been victimized "because of the thing with Hitler," for whom he indicated sympathy, and Jews in Israel for whom he felt "hatred" and against whom "he held a grudge." This strategy of separating the two groups enabled him to address the topic, which he clearly approached differently (having listed his sources of information as including "Arab books, and television series"), in terms of "sympathy" for Holocaust victims, while not giving up his personal stake and story as an exiled Palestinian.

This overt separation of the topic and the hesitation to talk openly about Israel is something that stood in stark contrast to replies and the group interviews with the visitors of upper-class West German background. So let us revisit this group of elites of West German origin and compare. On their questionnaire replies, a number of young men, who attested a great deal of background knowledge on the topic,[12] indicated a direct relationship between Jewish history in Germany and Israel. One of the most engaged young men wrote of his interest and expectations of the visit as follows:

> I think and I hope that I will learn some *new things* about the history of the Jews, I mean, further information, and not *only* about the persecution of the Jews during the Nazi time. So, for example, about the foundation of the state of Israel (underlining in the original) (QR 41, R 1.9). [His own feelings toward the topic, he related as]: I personally think that we Germans especially have a certain duty toward the Jews. And we may not suppress or forget our past. We must rather make sure that something like this can never happen again. We Germans have a duty toward the Jews that everyone should recognize! (QR 41, R 1.11)

After the visit, he voiced regret that his expectations were not completely fulfilled: "I found it a pity that there was little to nothing about the foundation of Israel to see. Also nothing about Herschel Grünspan, and information about Bengurion [*sic*] (Israel's founding father) was also missing" (QR 41, R 2.1). A classmate of his gave similar indications of such a direct connection between the topic and Israel. He wrote of his position as follows:

> Jewish life in Germany is formed by the Nazi destruction and extermination ma-
> nia, which has, in my view, welded Jewish cultural circles and their sympathizers
> closely together. That still today even Nazis use Jews as scapegoats for their own
> purposes is unbearable and fills me with shame. That people of the Jewish faith
> continue to wish to live here demands a great measure of my respect. I do worry
> about the increasingly spreading conflicts from the Middle East, in which some
> Palestinians, Lebanese, Syrians, among others, discredit Israel and deny its right
> to exist. Right-wing groups increasingly demonstrate solidarity with these groups,
> which I see as absolutely immoral! Israel's right to exist is and, for me, remains
> inviolable! (QR 42, R.1.11)

Both these young men voiced a direct link between their "German" guilt and solidarity with Jews and then afforded this to Israel as well. I was, at the time, quite surprised to find this so forcefully expressed by such young men. Perhaps it should have not surprised me. Indeed, conflation of Jews with Israel is hardly new. I did still find it remarkable that the first respondent expected to learn about Israel at the JMB. There seems to be a lack of knowledge that there is, in fact, a present-day Jewish presence in Germany. The visibility of institutions like the JMB, for example, stands in stark contrast to the invisibility of actual Jews living here.[13]

Since I found this expectation and the direct connection, expressed by these young men, interesting, I asked about this at the group interview. A lengthy discussion ensued (unlike in the *Neukölln* group where there had been silence). I begin:

> Regarding my question about how you deal with the past, what was relevant
> for you, many of you wrote: Anger over the past, terror and also a connection to
> present-day Israeli politics. How does one get from the Nazi time to present-day
> Israeli politics?

> [One of the engaged young men replies.]

> Yes, of course, when one is reminded of the history of the Jewish people, how they
> were expelled time and again, and especially now the Nazi time. Then it is clear that
> they have a very particular claim to their country ... I think that it very much ties
> back to the history. Nevertheless, in the exhibition, this modern aspect of Jewish
> history was missing—Israel, all the military altercations, the conflicts with Egypt
> and so on. This was somehow totally absent in the museum. The entire recent
> history, I would say, was missing. This was actually a real pity ... If one now says
> it, the Jewish museum, is a part of the culture of memory. Then I would say it has
> succeeded. But if one says: "I want the knowledge, to convey the history up to the
> present day." Then there is simply something missing, a level, as it were.

> [His classmate interjects.]

> I think, as far as modern Jewry, especially the state of Israel is concerned, it is like
> this: we Germans must never forget what has happened and now have and will

always have a special connection to Jewry and the state of Israel. This should not lead, in my opinion, automatically to unconditional support for Israel that we do not say: "Do whatever you want! We are for it!" only out of the fear, that we once had anti-Semitism … [inaudible]

Again about the statement that recent history and the reference to Israel was missing. Is that one thing for you, recent history of the Jews in Germany and Israel?

[The same young man replies directly.]

One cannot separate it, in my opinion.

It is directly connected with the German past and the Jewish past. That's why. That would also interest me. When one enters a Jewish museum, then one expects to also learn something about Israel. When one connects this. One does tie this together. Certainly, the main aspect is … this culture of memory is also okay too. Still, I think recent history would also be interesting for a museum and would also show this connection between Israel and Germany again more clearly: the responsibility and how it all came about. Then one might better understand it. Well, Israel does not exist because there was a country available there, but also, because these terrible things happened in Germany. And one cannot just separate this, in my view. The year 1933 relates too to the foundation of the state of Israel. Therefore, for me, this is part of one history.

[Now a young woman speaks up.]

I also wanted to say something: I read recently a study that said it was dangerous again, today to live in Berlin as a Jew—that just because of the history … I mean not because of the history, but because of the current events in and around Israel, that there is discrimination, as it were, here too. When I hear something like this, I find it really frightening. Even when it is now not coming from the Germans who live here. (TR 3 group interview 13 September 2007: 6–8)

There are certainly several noteworthy points brought up in this discussion: the assumption of a causal connection between the Holocaust and the founding of the State of Israel, and the view that German history and Israeli history is one unit, for example. Further, there was some reluctance with this group to criticize Israel. Recall, this class has also assumed I might be Jewish. Two participants offered mild criticisms of Israel (but only on the questionnaires). Both of these statements immediately preceded or followed by claims of Jewish antecedents. Consider, too the great care the members of this class took in their replies to me, one indicating that she had to be careful, especially in interactions with Jews on this topic (QR 39, R 1.11), and another writing that she felt exposed to accusations of anti-Semitism simply because she was German (QR 59, R 1.11). I am compelled to read these evocations of Jewish background as purposeful positioning aimed at allowing the speakers (writers in this case) some perceived freedom to criticize Israel, while avoiding possible accusations of anti-Semitism that might otherwise result from such criticism. I have also come to see these evocations of Jewishness as analogous to Mary Waters's concept of "ethnic options" whereby claiming a given ethnic background "does not limit the life possibilities" of those who can choose, as is the case for white middle class Americans who invoke Irish or Italian heritage (Waters 1990: 147). Indeed, the evocations of Jewish background by the young women are voluntary and do not effect their lives in negative ways. These children of upper–middle class German elites can claim a remote, partial Jewishness, based solely on blood ties, without giving up their status (Bishop Kendzia 2014: 64–65).

There was something else here that actually quite disturbed me in this lengthy and sophisticated interview. First, solidarity with Israel, which in itself need not be problematic, but here it was linked to the now overcome, one-time presence of anti-Semitism, hinted at by one of the young men. Second, the context of the young woman's expressed sympathy for the victims of anti-Semitism in Berlin today troubled me. While the sentiments themselves were indeed laudable, I found the context unsettling. What struck me was the framework of her discussion: she had been referring to reports of anti-Semitic acts carried out by Muslim youth living in Berlin. That such attacks are reprehensible is undebatable. It is their framing, however, that is problematic. She immediately and without hesitating described the anti-Semitic, Muslim aggressors as non-German. In her own words: "when I hear something like this, I find it really frightening. Even when it is now not coming from Germans who live here." So automatic and deep was the ethnic definition of Germanness. Further, the idea that anti-Semitism has been largely overcome by Germans of German background surprised me, given the various expressions of anti-Semitism emanating from the Far Left, and in mainstream society, not to mention several vicious attacks on Muslims that occur regularly (cf. Benz 2011; Bodemann 2002).

Characterizations of Muslims as the new and only anti-Semites are not uncommon in media and daily life, and just this came up, but only on paper, from the two young men in the Neukölln group, who had so stressed their own "German" credentials. In reply to feelings toward Jewish history in Germany, one wrote: "The Muslims should live in peace with the Jews. Otherwise none" (QR 63, R 1.11). While the other noted: "In Germany: no feelings (in the whole world: the Muslims should leave the Jews alone)" (QR 64, R 1.11). It is not impossible that they compared notes, but neither wanted to discuss this publicly, regardless. There was indeed far more hesitation to discuss these issues of anti-Semitism, Israel, and the Middle East with me from this group. This is again hardly surprising, considering the positionalities. The Muslim students might not have wanted to open themselves up to accusations of anti-Semitism, whereas the young men above might simply have preferred to avoid opening this can of worms, as it were, which may well have caused conflict in an otherwise harmonious class.

From Disorientation to Confusion versus Mastery

The mechanisms of exclusion be they in the museum, or beyond that I came to perceive led me to reflect further on the general culture that is producing this culture of memory as a dominant discourse, and to think again about my own situation here. I want to revisit here another situation in the museum and the classroom, which I found to have troubling implications that go beyond the culture of memory. Recalling how some of the young women had not had their questions adequately addressed in the museum, I turned to another episode of unmet needs that came up much earlier, during my first research session with a small grade twelve history class, a *Leistungskurs* (an advanced/extension course) from a lower–middle class area in what was once West Berlin.[14] This was with a group of eight pupils. The teacher, Mr L., was particularly engaged. Here is how I noted the meeting at the time.

This school is only a short bike ride away, and it is a warm summer day. Mr L. is friendly and open and says he likes the museum, especially for its architecture. He then takes my husband and me across a rather large outdoor courtyard to meet his pupils in the classroom. On the way to the classroom, a pleasant teenager, who from Mr L.'s reaction is clearly one of his students, appears and greets us just as we enter the building. He shakes my hand with confidence and says: "Hello, I'm Mehmet." He proceeds to explain that he is looking forward to the visit, as he is especially interested in the topic, because he is planning to write about the Armenian Genocide for his history term paper and wants to learn something about the Jewish experience in this museum. Wow, I think, that's pretty impressive. I reply that I find this very interesting and I hope he gets something out of the visit today. Mr L. mentions—as an aside to me—that he hopes Mehmet will manage his term paper, but he doesn't think he will since his German is not good enough. I am surprised at this: to my non-German ears, Mehmet's German sounded excellent. Indeed, he had been living in Germany for several years.[15]

They have all consented to taking part, and are respectful and listen as I explain what I want them to do. One young woman is smiling somewhat awkwardly as I talk, and I have the impression that she is trying to suppress a giggle, at my less than perfect German. I am used to this by now, though, as I have presented myself in flawed German on many occasions and have witnessed many a suppressed giggle. I must also admit that I was nervous during this: my very first introduction to a school group for the project, and assume that I likely made several mistakes.

As we descend the stairs to the underground axes, the kids are quiet, and once downstairs, a few view the displays with prolonged attention. They are reading the signage. Others read the large printed texts on the walls and proceed along slowly. This lasts some time with some spending several minutes at a display. They seem to spend the most time looking and reading about artifacts left behind by murdered children. A young woman asks me for directions. Where to go next? The group tends to want to be guided and stays together with one exception: a young woman, who has been to the museum on two previous occasions, goes off on her own directly to the stairs toward the upper floors. Mr L. had pointed her out to me earlier as his star pupil, Kerstin. I note too that it was she, who I recall had tried to suppress the giggle during my initial introduction.

I remain with the group as they turn down the Axis of the Holocaust continuing to read the signage and look at the displays. They move slowly, their body language is reserved, even a bit timid. One young woman mentions the strange feeling under her feet, and the contrast between the dark floor and the light walls makes her feel strange. At the displays along the walls, they peer into the glass but stand quite rigid, most with arms crossed in front of their chests. The group also seems a bit disoriented, and two ask if there is anything else they should look at down here. They are both first-time visitors and do want some direction. I recommend the Axis and Garden of Exile. They want to be led, so I lead them there. It is a lovely day, and we go outside among the pillars and slanted ground. Here they are again a bit louder, but still reserved and respectful, walking among the pillars. One complains she is getting nauseous. Mehmet who is also walking among the pillars asks me why it is built like this. I echo the caption that appears on the wall before one enters, in which we are asked to experience the disorientation that exile brings. A feeling of no solid ground under your feet, of being uncomfortable in your path. The group all listen to my short explanation. I get the impression that they are not satisfied from facial expressions (furled brows, perplexed expressions).

Later, we enter the first section of the permanent exhibition. Almost immediately, the mood seems to shift. Their body language is more relaxed, they chat in a conversational easy tone. Smiles appear on their faces, and they then proceed to ask questions. What is this tree? Can we write wishes? I tell them, of course, go ahead. They spend a lot of time at the tree, climbing up the steps surrounding the tree, with quick bouncing movements, filling out their wishes, reading other wishes already on the tree. They all wrote wishes.

I accompany the group through the next sections, where they often use the interactives, like the Glikl packing game. I notice Kerstin there. She was spending a lot of time looking at a model of a synagogue and then at one of the adjacent computer terminals. She soon went off again on her own. The group spends quite some time in these next sections, writing words in Hebrew. By the time we get to the section on the establishment of modern Judaism, it is almost time to go, as we have only allotted two and a half hours for this visit. Clearly more time will have to be made for future visits.

Some of the visitors complain that it is over and want to see more. Others seem happy to finish and seem tired. "Oh well," says one of the young women, "We'll have to come back again soon."

As we gathered at the meeting point on the ground floor, I handed out the post-visit questionnaires. Mr L. is there waiting for us. He did not tour the museum with us, but will be there during the interview. They took a few minutes to fill them in. This they did individually without consulting each other. Then we proceed outside around back, where there were benches, so we could talk about the visit together and I could ask them about their impressions (Field diary 22 June 2007).[16]

During the group interview, a number of issues were raised including confusion and the need for more direction. Mehmet was particularly vocal on these points:

> I think one needs a guide. For a museum like this one needs a guide. It is built very strangely, I find, very strangely. Well, I didn't really learn anything about the history of the Jews … not really, means nothing at all! I think it's good that they wanted to distance themselves from the Holocaust, because one can go elsewhere if one wants to learn what happened. But, generally one does not learn about anything else. But instead, there's a lot about biographies of individual people. One should have simply constructed the museum according to a time line … that one can go through chronologically from the beginning up to today. (TR 1 group interview 22 June 2007)

Mehmet was not satisfied with this visit. And clearly, it will not help him with his history paper on the Armenian genocide. He had indicated a fair amount of background knowledge on the topic as follows: "In history class in grade nine. I have also visited concentration camps. Television reports, books." And interest "above all, in the history of the Jews during the Third Reich." He was, as he mentioned in the interview, very disappointed "since one could learn only little without a tour" and wrote that "nothing sparked my interest" (QR 1, R 1.10, 1.11, 2.7, 2.9). He, and most of his group in fact, would certainly have benefited from a dedicated tour, perhaps even one that may have touched on issues related to his own particular interest in the Armenian topic. Thus, although his needs were not met within this freely framed visit to the museum, it is not unlikely that the museum could meet such needs if specific requests were made.

Let us contrast his position with Kerstin's. Remember, she had toured the museum confidently and independently. She did not speak up during the interview, but did note her impressions on her questionnaire replies.[17] She had indicated very high interest in the topic and a wide variety of sources of background knowledge: "In the Jewish museum, in history class, from my grandfather and children of concentration camp prisoners, friends who live in/come from Israel." Her feelings, she noted as: "I find it terrible that one group has been the scapegoat of German history over centuries. This crime cannot be made good again." Regarding the underground sections, she noted: "The Garden of Exile was structured in an exciting way, so slanted. Because of the emptiness in the tower one could contemplate the events well." But also criticized it: "I do not find, however, that it reflected the Holocaust well." The museum's significance to her personally was "a very big one, one must not forget what happened" (QR 7, R 1.10, 1.11, 2.3, 2.5). Kerstin indicates and embodies a clear mastery of the topic and the museum, even offering a rather sophisticated critique.

As I reflected further on the contrast between Mehmet and Kerstin's experience of the museum, certain issues came to preoccupy me: the different way their teacher had described them to me, for example. Kerstin was his star pupil, clearly at home in the classroom, much as she had been in the JMB. She mastered the exhibition well—just as she was at home in the language, so much so that she could not suppress a giggle at my far-less-than-perfect German. Whereas Mehmet, for all his interest in the subject matter, is, according to his teacher who has the power to decide, unlikely to be able to complete his course qualification, and thereby the *Abitur*, due to his poor German language skills—which are clearly much better than mine. Thus, while his needs vis-à-vis the museum might be easily met by a specific tour, his broader educational needs may not be quite so easy to tackle.

Language and Participation—
An Auto-Ethnography with Wider Implications

What might the implications of this illustration be? In order to situate my analysis of this episode, I think a more in-depth auto-ethnographic approach is necessary. Further, the issues I am about to explore revolve very much around the differences between practices I grew up with in Canada, and those that have come to form and inform my impressions living in Berlin.

I must admit that this realization of Mehmet's language disadvantage was quite a shock and wake-up call to me personally, as someone who has worked extensively with new Canadians in Toronto getting their English language skills up to the level necessary for university admittance. If Canadian institutions were as fussy about English as it seems to be the case with German here, then nonnative speakers could not expect to participate fully in Canadian society. I wondered that there were not measures already in place to make sure that Mehmet's German was good enough for him, an intelligent and engaged pupil, to complete the *Abitur.* Remember he had been here several years already.

I have since come to see how deeply this issue of language and participation—or lack thereof—runs, even in very sympathetic environments. What follows is an exploration of a situation I encountered as a teaching assistant in a project seminar at my university institute. The project involved going into junior high school classes in areas of Berlin with a high immigrant background population and working with the young pupils using ethnographic methods.

Today I gave a very short presentation to the class, in German of course, introducing myself and explaining what I do as an ethnologist to the grade seven pupils. As I spoke, I noticed that one girl expressed surprise to hear that I was from Canada. Later on in a short discussion with a master's student in the seminar [who was also part of the project], *I discover that I came up there in an exchange. One pupil, who had recently come to Germany from Bulgaria, had expressed surprise that someone who did not speak perfect German could teach at a university! What a different world! I thought. I remember many of my teachers in high school, and later university whose accents were so strong that I and the other pupils had to struggle to understand them at first* (Field diary 7 June 2010).

I then recalled that when we were deciding who would explain ethnology to the pupils, Paul (a colleague who was initially interested in the project) said that I should not do it, because my accent might disturb the pupils. I had not thought of this. I asked him if he might prefer to do it. I was happy to defer the task to him, but he did not want the job. The ethnology master's students were also not so keen on doing this. Both the professor leading the project seminar, and one of the project founders proclaimed that my accent was no barrier to my giving the introduction. Therefore, in the end I did, as mentioned, give the presentation.

Paul's comment did make me feel a bit insecure about my accent. Consequently, I asked the professor again what he thought about the effect of my accent. With a warm and encouraging smile, he said: "It's actually very endearing, like a slight handicap." This threw me for a loop! "I am in the wrong movie," I thought. This was especially troubling to me as there was no malice in the comment, and the professor has been supportive of my work, giving much of his time to it, in an academic environment where professors have very limited time capacity. It was he who invited me to coteach the seminar in question, and he has repeatedly encouraged me to participate in academic life at the institute, making me feel at home there. I trust and do believe that his view of how my accent might be perceived is very likely accurate, which of course, makes it all the more painful. It had never occurred to me that an accent might be perceived as a handicap. I am not sure I liked the idea that listeners are pitying me: the poor woman with her "handicap." I much rather hope that they attend to the content of what I am saying. My mind ventured briefly to the idea of Hannah Arendt lecturing in Chicago and her German accident being viewed as a handicap.

It remains important to ask: what are the implications of such expectations of language proficiency for growing a sense of belonging here among immigrants to Germany? Indeed, in order to belong one has to imagine a place. And tangibly a place also means the prospect of education and employment. In this light, the possibility of Mehmet's not being given the opportunity to complete the *Abitur* is highly problematic. As expected, when I met his teacher again quite some time later, he told me that he had, in fact, failed Mehmet, not only due to language weaknesses, but also because his treatment of the Armenian genocide issue was too close to the official Turkish national position. In considering Mehmet's situation, it is useful to recall Schiffauer and Baumann's findings, mentioned in the previous chapter, that civil enculturation is largely implicit in Germany. It is quite likely that Mehmet (like the young women who had asked why the Jews had not converted to avoid death) was not given explicit guidance. He would have needed such guidance to pass. Moreover, and more problematically, the education system does not take responsibility for making sure their pupils of many years have sufficient German language skills, which they need to thrive.[18] This deficiency is compounded by the expectation of accent-free language skills. Becoming reasonably fluent in a new language is one thing and is a realistic, and indeed an integrative, goal. Mastering the language to the extent that one is perceived as a native speaker and has no accent is another issue altogether; it would be an unreachable assimilatory expectation. If the latter is viewed as a necessary prerequisite for inclusion and participation—even the kind of small participation that Paul thought I should not undertake—then I can see how discouraging and counterproductive this habitus regarding the German language might be. Further, it seems to me quite incompatible in practice with the situations on the ground in Berlin—a city shaped by cultural diversity and global networks and relationships. Fundamental educational reform is certainly required. Moreover, work would also have to be done to convince a critical mass of the voting public, that such reform is good, as in pragmatically preferable, for the country as whole.

This journey in and around the museum began and now comes to an end as a very personal one, during which I sought to better understand the culture of memory in which I find myself and my family. Now, it is time to gather the many impressions and analyses, and pull together the most crucial lessons and implications.

Notes

1. These two young men emphasized their "Germanness" on the questionnaires, which in this case did not remain anonymous, as they showed them to me at the time, stressing their choice of pseudonyms with pride: one had chosen to call himself "Hertha BSC" (the Berlin professional football team). One listed nationality, native language, and religion as follows: "GERMAN!, GERMANY!, PROTESTANT!" The other as, "GERMAN!, GERMAN!, No [religion]." The use of the capitals (not to mention exclamation marks) was striking as the rest of their replies only had capital letters and punctuation where they would normally be used (QR 63 and 64, R 1.3–1.5). In contrast to the school groups from the upper–middle class areas of Berlin, which I had mentioned were almost entirely made up of Germans of German background, this class of twenty-four had only three pupils who claimed German background. The other twenty-one all noted that they and/or their parents were from countries other than Germany such as Turkey, Iraq, Palestine, and Pakistan. It also struck me that those of Turkish background who indicated that they had one German parent and German citizenship nevertheless described themselves as exclusively Turkish (QR 65, R 1.3). While others who noted that they had German citizenship, wrote that they were "German on paper" but actually "Turkish—Kurdish," for example (QR 69, R 1.39). Such ambivalence toward German citizenship is not unusual (cf. Mandel 2008).

2. I remember an episode at the Holocaust Memorial earlier that summer when some young visitors were playing hide and seek there among the stelae, while others were sitting on the lower stelae eating packed lunches. This behavior was not unusual. I noticed some older visitors looking very grumpy and leaving in a huff. I assumed from their conversation that they were likely Americans. I approached them and asked them if anything was wrong? They looked so upset, maybe I could help them, I asked? The woman explained that she was really offended by how the kids here disrespected these graves, sitting on them, playing and running, and laughing. "Don't they realize that these are the graves for our ancestors who were murdered?" She was almost in tears, she was so angry. I was lost for words and could only offer a meekly delivered

explanation that the kids probably do not think of the stelae as graves at all, but rather just as pillars open to many interpretations, much as the creator of this memorial described them. I explain that visitors often sit on them without meaning to give offense. The couple expresses surprise that they were not always seen as graves. They are still upset, though. I also find myself wanting to apologize for the kids, but I resist this impulse as I do not actually think they did anything wrong. The couple leave, a bit less upset maybe, but do say that the kids should still be more sensitive to other visitors. I recall to myself that I too automatically see the stelae as symbolic graves. I can never quite bring myself to sit on them. Still the conflict that this varying interpretation, but the assumption of a common one, brings is worth keeping in mind (Field diary 22 June 2007). Indeed, if an interpretation, or memory for that matter, is assumed to be common and so made normative, when it is in fact not common at all, then the normativity can well create conflict, and be oppressive, especially to those who do not share the expected interpretation.

3. I should mention that at the time I did not recognize the song. It is not as if one hears the national anthem regularly here (unlike in my own elementary school where we sang the Canadian national anthem every morning standing as the tune was piped in the classroom through the intercom). After Mr R. had asked them to stop singing, I went to the loudest singer, the young woman who had spoken such excellent English, and asked her what she had been singing. "The German national anthem," she replied with a smile and an air of mischief in her voice.

4. This was confirmed, for example, in informal conversations with Holocaust Tower attendants in November and June 2007, and in a more formal interview with a member of the Education Department staff on 24 February 2011. Further, after this very clearly expressed confusion, and another review of several questionnaire replies from other visitors, it does seem that a number may well have had a similar interpretation of the tower, but it was expressed more subtly. They did not ask the staff about it, and it did not lead to any visible conflicts. For example: two young women of West German background, from a lower–middle class area, had written of the Holocaust Tower as "very depressing and cold. Unimaginable that Jews were imprisoned there" (QR 4, R 2.3), and "pretty awful! Imagining that Jews were imprisoned there" (QR 5, R 2.3).

5. I was left wondering how the reaction by teachers and museum staff might have been quite different had the singers of the national anthem in front of the JMB been perceived as Germans of German background. This, though, would have to remain speculation, as I have not seen this happen in my many, many visits there.

6. A general lack of interest in this topic on the part of Germans of Arab and Turkish background is well-attested in literature (cf. Margalit 2009), by practitioners in the field, such as tour guides at the JMB (cf. Kouparanis 2008). It seems then that the class that was recommended to me was in this sense exceptional as many members did express much interest in the topic.

7. As I mentioned previously, this is not unlike the replies that many Germans of Turkish background gave in my study. This is something that was also alien to me at the time, referring to someone or to oneself as a migrant or a foreigner even after two or more generations of your family have lived here.

8. G: Also, das kam von der Schule aus … Da war ich halt der einzige aus unserer Klasse. Die anderen hat es eigentlich nicht so interessiert. … Hat, wie gesagt, fünfzig Prozent Deutsche in der Klasse, und ich war der einzige Ausländer sozusagen, der sich dafür interessiert hat.

9. Georgi, Viola B. 2003 *Entliehene Erinnerung. Geschichtsbilder junger Migranten in Deutschland.* Hamburg: Hamburger Edition.
   Dabei haben ja viel geweint und alles. Die hat das ganz schön mitgenommmen. Also mir ging's, mir war's da nicht zum Weinen zumute … Natürlich ist es traurig, ich mein' / ich würde ja auch nicht gerne so leben / na ja, und als ich da gesagt hab': "Warum weint ihr denn eigentlich? Ihr müßt nicht drüber weinen, denkt drüber nach." Da kam schon wieder dieses: "Eh, du als Ausländer, du hast doch keine Ahnung." [He then continues.] Und das is' ein Punkt gewesen, wo ich micht aufgeregt hab', weil ich kann das nicht akzeptieren (*erregt gestikulierend*) Erstens: Ich durfte nicht hierher kommen. Ich bin hier geboren. Zweitens: ich hab den deutschen Paß. Drittens: Ich sprech' die Sprache perfekt. … Ich fühl mich hier nicht als Ausländer. Irgendwo bin ich auch ein Deutscher, aber irgendwo auch türkisch. Ich bin beides.

10. As mentioned in Chapter 3, these young participants did, however, emphasize their Germanness, and that the JMB was approached differently from other *national* perspectives (the French, for example).

11. These insights are also explored in Bishop Kendzia 2012.

12. The sources of information listed ranged from conversations with parents and grandparents, to several visits to relevant memorial sites, to many books and films (indeed some of these young visitors listed so many sources that it could hardly fit on the page).

13. I explore this impression that Jews in Germany exist only in the past at some length in Bishop Kendzia 2010: 48–49. The invisibility of present-day Jews in Germany is also well attested in literature (cf. Bodemann 1996). I would just note here that this view was not only documented throughout the questionnaire replies, but also in the museum itself: I would occasionally overhear guides asking visitors to estimate the number of Jews in Germany before 1933, and again to guess how many live in Germany now. Invariably, the earlier estimates were largely inflated, going well above several million, while the present-day guesses fell far short of even the most conservative estimates. Generally, the official number of pre-1933 Jews in Germany is given as ca. 500,000. Present-day figures range from official Jewish community member numbers as 106,000 to much larger numbers, which can be many times that. Lately, on a documentary on *Deutschlandfunk* (National German Radio), I heard a figure of ca. 20,000 Israeli Jews in Berlin alone. These numbers would not be reflected in official Jewish community figures.

14. Specifically, a *Leistungskurs* subject is chosen by the pupil and is one that has double the number of hours per week of other courses. The choice of this subject is significant as the *Abitur* exam will then not only contain a test on it (in this case history), but also because the final *Abitur* grade will also be weighted heavily by the grade in the class work in the subject.

15. Mehmet was the only nonnative German speaker in the group, and the only one of Turkish background. One of the young women had Italian parents; the other six pupils were German of West German background. Mehmet did, however, indicate his nationality as German. This was in fact quite exceptional among the questionnaire replies, as I have already mentioned: the vast majority of Germans of Turkish background described themselves as Turkish.

16. Unlike the later visits, in this case, the group interview was held immediately following the visit at the museum itself. It was quite exhausting both for the participants and for myself. Therefore, I decided it would be better to have a few days break between the visit and the group interview.

17. In this small group, the questionnaires did not remain anonymous and the pupils did not want this, and even gave real names, which I have altered for publication purposes.

18. Although a thorough exploration of the structural inequalities in the German school system is, as I have previously mentioned, beyond the scope of this book, it is important to highlight here, the obstacles that the implicitness of the educational process create. Implicit expectations pose a challenge to inclusion. My own personal experience also suggests that little has changed: now that both my daughters are going through the secondary school system in Berlin (both at *Gymnasien*), I see clearly that expectations are rarely ever explained. It is just expected that the parents will tell their children what is to be done. While my husband and I, educated in the liberal arts and privileged, possess this knowledge, not everyone does. Those pupils who do not have access to the German language at home, have a particularly difficult time, often never making it to *Gymnasien*. Those children of non-German speakers who are in my daughters' schools (they go to two different schools), for example, have had years of paid after-school tutoring with both their parents working full time to accomplish this.

Chapter 6

CONCLUDING REFLECTIONS

From the Museum as a Field Site
to a More Inclusive Culture of Memory

On Engagement and Political Correctness—
Between Political Confirmation and Holocaust Fatigue

Clearly, that I have been able to carry out this work and found so many engaged interlocutors is a testament to the continued relevance of the topic and the significance of the JMB in and around the school curricula. Indeed, visitors engaged in varying ways with the building itself and the exhibitions housed therein, often expressing empathetic interest in the topic and the museum. Difficulties and challenges were also made especially visible, since as a field site, the museum also reflected tendencies prevailing in the culture of memory and the more general culture in Germany.

A number of these tensions were illustrated in the very makeup of the museum and the positioning that followed: first choosing the *Libeskind-Bau,* then claiming, and asserting in words and other practices, to not be a Holocaust museum. Let us recall that the conception of the JMB, as it now stands, was in the hand of West German elites of a generation now far removed from those pupils who partook in this present study. This latter assertion of not being a Holocaust museum becomes entangled with the issue of Holocaust fatigue. Wolfgang Kaschuba not only casts serious doubt on the presence of a shared memory of the Nazi past, but also questions the continued relevance of the memorial forms and symbols for the younger generations today. He also stresses the need to negotiate new avenues, which might be more receptive to their needs (Kaschuba 2005: 195). These insights are confirmed throughout the material I have gathered.

Even though I was led in my study to do research on, and with, very interested young visitors and many, most notably those children of elites, embodied a dominant discourse of *Betroffenheit,* the problem of an exhaustion with the expected performance of "guilt," nevertheless, became visible.[1] This dynamic rather than constituting a contradiction, as it may appear at first glance, links being habituated to the discourse of *Betroffenheit* directly to the problem of a compulsion to perform, which seems to operate within the sphere of political education here. Consider the young man of upper–middle class, West German background who so eloquently spoke of his own approach to this past linking it to guilt and yet would like now to have access to a Jewish museum where the Holocaust was left out altogether. Reflect on the classmate's statement that he had:

> the feeling that the German-Jewish past generates the compulsion to have to dedicate oneself exclusively, especially in the years just preceding high school, to literature and books for young people about the Jewish problematic. As a result, other educational materials are withheld from the pupils, for example in German class. (QR 32, R 1.11)

These critiques are coming from insiders, operating within the dominant code. The structures, the symbols, and ways of approaching this past, are not working for them fully.

The JMB as a stage seems then to be functioning, within this context, as site of flawed political confirmation for these already-initiated insiders, as opposed to teaching them anything new—or politically educating them as such. In approaching the situations with them, Sharon Macdonald's concept of the indeterminacy of performance is also a useful framework. It may be that the constellations I found myself in with these young visitors represented more or less superficial performances, at times. It may also be that much of what was said and written was genuinely felt. The binary of either/or is not particularly helpful, and in any case would not essentially alter the end analysis here. There is something fundamentally amiss with the culture of memory, as it pertains to political education, either way: if such feelings of guilt and shame, for example, are truly felt, it is problematic since such sentiments are out of place and unsustainable for all but those who actually committed the crimes. If such feelings are not really felt, but merely presented, it is equally problematic, for then the compulsion to perform such a disconnected affect is what is out of place and alienating, although it may still serve to bind a superficially "guilty We-Group" together, to the exclusion of others. I come to this again shortly.

Reflecting further on the implications of Wolfgang Kaschuba's observations that there is "no archive of a shared memory" (2005: 196) on the topic and my own journey within it. I find myself in the midst of a very paradoxical environment. I would break it down as follows: there seems to be a lack of actually shared memory on the topic. Add to this a strongly performative guilt trope, which came into being well after the fact, spearheaded by socio-intellectual elites of the generation that came after 1945. This trope has been articulated in statements such as "Germany is the land of the perpetrators" touched on already. Moreover, it is performed by younger generations well into the present at sites like the JMB. All this in the absence of any solid foundation of a perpetrator narrative on the part of the actually guilty.

In considering this, I am reminded of Edward Herman and Noam Chomsky's 1988, now famous, critique of the U.S. mass media that argues consent has to be manufactured in democracies, rather than overtly and obviously imposed from above, for it to be at all sustainable. Their critique of U.S. media itself is a much bigger topic than cannot be addressed here. Indeed, arguing the merits of their position is well beyond the scope of this work. My point is more that coercion is evident in and around the museum: the carefully considered replies, the times when visitors were admonished for failing to demonstrate *Betroffenheit,* even the subtler admissions that such affective displays are expected of "Germans" at such sites, actual feelings notwithstanding.

I wonder whether this disconnect, as well as the unsustainability of guilt *per se,* might be part of the reason that the *Betroffenheit* mode has so often become oppressive, and miseducative, for its practitioners. So much in the museum behavior specifically, and the culture of memory generally, from my reading of the young visitors' language (written, spoken, and gestural) seems to indicate that this form of remembrance is as much, if not more, about not so subtle coercion then about any real consensus. I would further argue that any political educational endeavor based so strongly on overt pressure, is indeed bound to fail in a democratic environment.

From this point of view, the coercion thrown into sharp relief with these sophisticated rememberers runs counter to democratic tendencies. Whether it be, the pressure visitors expressed about expectations to perform in a certain way in the museum, or the hapless reactions of those who were admonished and did not know why. How can one hope to teach moral courage, for example, in an environment where the students do not feel free to speak their minds? Should a democratic environment not try to foster a space where people can believe, feel, and speak with a certain sense of freedom?

On High-Level Politicization—The Culture of Memory as an Instrument of Power

Overt political instrumentalization of the topic was visible at the gala exhibition opening among many other media events too numerous to mention. That the museum also fulfills public relations functions was also not lost on many of the visitors in my study, when they expressed pride in having such a great memorial-museum in Berlin, which is then a signpost for Germany, showing it in a good light. The larger culture of memory based on particular national positioning and *Betroffenheit* toward this past has also been used as an instrument of power. It can be used to tell other nations how best to remember this and their past and/or to defend Germany from accusations of racism or even, more problematically, to occlude present-day racisms and recast Muslims as the new, especially anti-Semitic, threat (cf. El-Tayeb 2016: 181–82; Partridge 2010: 822, 2015: 13). This threat is also portrayed in such a way that just happens to envision German elites, with their memory of Nazism as its best-equipped counter (El-Tayeb 2016: 171). The young museum visitors who showed outrage over anti-Semitism perpetrated by "non Germans" or wrote, "that the Muslims should leave the Jews alone" were clearly tapping into this larger political discourse.

On Confusion and Exclusion

The museum as a field site also reflected more general tendencies of the West over East domination that followed the German "unification" and troubling exclusions from national belonging experienced by Germans of Turkish and Arab background.

The conflicts in and around the museum that occurred with those groups of visitors who did not perform appropriately were very illustrative. The situations in which the museum visit occasion was not characterized by *Betroffenheit* produced telling reactions: those who had been read as German of German background, were thereby required/expected to behave in line with the assumed universal Holocaust memorial occasion. They were expected to sing along with their mostly elite West German counterparts, the most accomplished choral singers. When they did not, it caused offense. While those who had been read as somehow more different, such as the *Neukölln* group, while they were at times scolded, were more problematically disregarded and shut out of the conversation, quite literally: seen as silly, rather than offensive. Damani Partridge has also touched on similar tendencies in his empirical work, which included a youth group trip to Auschwitz, with Berlin-based pupils of Turkish and Palestinian background. He recalls the following:

> Just before leaving Auschwitz, the foundation liaison asked me to tell the group more about my work. I talked about how impressed I was with how loving and

close-knit the group was. Later, however, it occurred to me that this community was ephemeral, a temporary form of community made tighter by a new experience of trauma that would tie them more to each other, but not to the nation-state that wanted them also to remember. The foundation liaison worried about his participation in nation building, but then quickly added that for these youth that was not the point. The point of the state-funded program was simply to make them less irritating residents within the nation-state, not, the logic follows, to make them more equal members who would be given a larger platform from which to speak, even to their experience in relation, if not in comparison, to this history. (Partridge 2010: 848)

The implications of such situations are worrisome. They continue to preoccupy me personally. While I was impressed to see the creative agency that the young women displayed in the museum in order to finally get their questions addressed, the resignation of many in the group to the exclusionary treatment and the more generally taken-for-granted continued ethnic definition of Germanness have caused me to temper my optimism. Countering these general tendencies to exclude, which are otherwise simply reflected in the museum, would require deliberate and confident action. It may be that this is already under way within other initiatives, even those at the JMB, like the tours offered by Muslim tour guides, also in Turkish, which highlight similarities between Judaism and Islam (Feldman and Peleikis 2014; Kouparanis 2008). Another example is the "JMB on tour" project, which travels to sites like youth detention centers to teach about Jewish culture (Lenhardt 2009).

In 2012, the museum added an academic program that specifically aims to foster diversity. This includes expert conferences open to the public that explore topics such as migration, anti-Semitism, and Islamophobia, for example. They operate at a very high, cutting-edge scholarly level. With such initiatives, the museum leadership has shown that it both recognizes problems of exclusion and marginalization in society, and that there is a will to counter these. Any wider success would depend, however, on building competencies throughout the museum.

In a recent conversation with a JMB staff member, who is involved with the academic program, I outlined the problems these visitors had encountered. She expressed surprise at first, but then went on the say that the museum has good intentions, but sometimes the competencies are not there. She mentioned that the guides tended to be very aware and sensitive. Additionally, they were well paid for their work. The lower level staff (like those who attend the Holocaust Tower and the coat check), on the other hand, were paid next to nothing and not trained, as such. I would argue then that priority should be given to choosing, training, and keeping

diverse staff, who do embody core competencies of empathy.[2] It is important to recall that such small acts of practice, that expose how difference is
understood and managed, can so influence visitor experience and potentially counteract well-intentioned programming. I would argue that more
focus and funds should be dedicated to supporting staff members who are
in a position to communicate directly with the museum's many publics.

Conflated Terms: "Cultural Pluralism" and "Integration"

In thinking about the inclusion of diversity in Germany, I need to recall
my initial confusion over terms. I would often see these words "cultural
pluralism" and "integration" in German scholarly literature (and of course
in media), but in ways quite contrary to the understanding of them I myself had internalized. This resulted in much confusion on my part. I would
wonder at the use of the word "integration," for example, when what was
actually being talked or written about was what I understood as "assimilation." I would look in vain to perceive a "culturally pluralistic" Germany
that was so much the topic of discussion. I hope in this next section to
spare other interlocutors, who also want to communicate internationally
in Germany and beyond, some of the bewilderment I suffered in Berlin.

I start with my implicit understanding of the term "cultural pluralism."
It is connected with how the term itself was originally coined in a partic-
ular place and time, namely in America in the early twentieth century.
Barbara Kirshenblatt-Gimblett offers a summary of this history:

> About a million immigrants were arriving annually, and revolution and war in
> Europe guaranteed a continuous flood of new refugees. The Treaty of Versailles, at
> the end of World War I, would redraw the European map and attempt to guaran-
> tee the rights of national minorities within newly created republics in central and
> eastern Europe. With American nationalism on the rise, "inassimilable aliens" on
> American soil saw their national aspirations fostered in Europe even as they faced
> increasing hostility in America: conservative intellectuals who envisioned a great
> melting pot or aimed to preserve the superiority of Anglo-American superiority
> had little patience with the foreigners in their midst. In opposition to them, lib-
> eral intellectuals such as Horace Kallen, who coined the term "cultural pluralism,"
> and Randolf Bourne, who proposed a "transnational America," condemned the
> position that immigrants should be stripped of their "ancestral endowment" and
> proposed instead that cultural differences be respected as part of "American civili-
> zation." (Kirshenblatt-Gimblett 1998: 112)

This positioning by the American liberal intellectuals at the time also had
influence on the Canadian model, which eventually rejected the assimi-

lative melting pot image. Indeed, I understood these terms as they were used in a settler-colony context, which constructed itself from the onset as an "immigration country" where the situation is, in this context, so very different.[3] Trying to apply such terms without necessary qualifications (I would actually urge scholars here to find new terms that do not cause such confusion and conflations) is highly problematic for a number of reasons. To me a viable practice of cultural pluralism means that a critical mass of the population accepts and recognizes difference as belonging to its nation or group.

My journey through the JMB and in the schools with the pupils demonstrates that this is far from the case: hard boundaries are set and strengthened between Germans and all the "others," including Jews and residents of Turkish background, regardless of citizenship and/or place of birth. The culture of memory as one based on rejecting the Nazi past remains closed to all but ethnic Germans, as Dan Diner (1998) also found. Indeed, the *Neukölln* group was not expected or given guidance on how to perform, just told to behave. To be "less irritating," much like those encountered by Damani Partridge. This indicates a segregation process at work, which is reinforced by an education system that relies on implicit knowledge. Consequently, norms and expectations are very difficult for newcomers or outsiders to access. The flip side of this are the assimilative expectations that were evident: let us consider the young visitors of East German background, who had behaved as tourists generally do, and gotten scolded as a result. They were expected to behave, and feel, just like the other "Germans." No space was made for difference. It was simply not tolerated. Further, the young women in question realized that they needed to gain more knowledge on the topic. They bombarded me with questions wanting a "way in," a means of comprehending the museum, specifically and the topic, more generally.

What follows now are my struggles surrounding further assimilative tendencies that arose over time. Here, I find it appropriate and indeed important to venture into the realm of auto-ethnography.

Assimilation—Between Self-Amputation and Impossibility

As I made clear in the preface, I began with a desire to connect my own multiple belongings, and my hope to raise my children in a balanced way, with exploring how the memory of the Nazi past is approached here. This was one of the original impetuses for my beginning to explore this topic. My daughters go to school here and are also exposed to the dominant culture of memory, not only to my own take on the history and my mother's, their grandmother's, story. They seem to be generally accepted members of the mainstream. Quite some time ago now, as my eldest daughter was about to begin learning about the Nazi period in history in her grade five class, she expressed much excitement: "Yay, I can't wait to learn about it!" This enthusiasm I thought might be connected to the fact that I too have been focusing on parts of this topic for most of her conscious existence. Occasionally, she would be exposed to discussions between my husband and I, and I did take my daughters to the JMB more than once, so that they could "finally see what Mommy was working on."

A few weeks later, after she had started to cover the topic in class, she came home one day, ran past me, went straight to her father, and exclaimed in German (which she speaks with her father), with a wry smile on her face: "Daddy, we are the worst criminals in the world, aren't we?" He asked what she had meant: "Well, we started the World War I, then II, and what with the Holocaust." My husband then tried to situate her within these events explaining that she was not even born when all this happened, that neither was he. And her grandparents had been small children then. I then entered the conversation: "Whoa! Who do you mean by 'we'?," I asked. She had meant "We Germans," of course. This was part of the reason her father was included, and I was not. I explain that she has many We-Groups she could choose to invoke. "But I'm German," she argued back, this time speaking to me in German. A lot went through my mind at the time. But what bothered me the most was the realization that in order to belong here to the dominant We-Group, my daughter had, if only for a moment, to forget her Jewish grandmother, or even her English antecedents, for that matter. This construction she came home from school with: "We are the worst criminals in the world" was an assimilatory one that did not make room for difference. Clearly, it is the construction that is the problem, not the multiple belongings my children might potentially have access to.

I then started to doubt myself as a parent: had I not given my daughter access to other possibilities? Indeed taking her to Canada more than the one trip we made, is beyond our means, and the few trips to England to visit family are clearly not enough. The Jewish issue is more complicated. I myself was not raised Jewish and just do not see that I should start instilling a sort of Jewishness in my daughter. She knows her grandmother, knows her story. Further, I did and do not want to take away her sense of belonging to the big, powerful, We-Group here, which seems to stand in opposition to a Jewish sense of self.

This assimilatory dilemma also came up in another situation. This time in relation to my research. I got an e-mail from a young woman, Tanya, who was interested in discussing my work as she wanted to do something similar for her masters here at a quite renowned university with one of the top professors in Germany. So, I met her for a drink one day, and it was very pleasant. I went over my findings on the still prevalent discourse of guilt among the children of West German intellectual elites. She then replied to me right away: "It is really very influential." She then continued, recounting that her parents had come from Russia when she had been a small child. Her mother had worked as a house cleaner. Tanya liked it in Germany and considered herself German. She is fluent in German. "Now at the university," she explained, "I am moving in circles where this guilt comes up and I start to feel guilty too. And then I have to slap myself and say: 'Wait, I am Jewish!' It is so weird." My reading of this situation is that, she would like to belong and be "German," but this guilt trope does not make it possible for her. Unlike my daughter's situation, Tanya cannot claim a German parent, but is willing and able to embrace her Jewishness. In the light of the fieldwork in and around the museum, both my daughter's and Tanya's situations make sense. The visitors perceived hard boundaries between Germans as perpetrators and Jews either as victims or as quaint exotic others. It is hardly a surprise then that my eldest daughter chose the one in-group over the other outside group, and that Tanya found herself in the bizarre situation of starting to feel like she belongs to the in-group, then being snapped out of it. Such separations and essentialisms are reinforced in the museum, as they are in the grade five classroom and Tanya's university circles. Those small findings that had puzzled me at the time: children with one German and one Turkish parent, indicating that they were Turkish rather than German, for example, not to mention those who, despite German citizenship, did not claim Germanness hit home, literally.

Toward a Recognized Diversity

Clearly moving beyond the concept of an ethno-national sense of belonging, for those who are ready and willing to do this, necessitates the letting go of the guilt or atonement-based culture of memory and replacing it with something new. Perhaps that something might involve what Viola Georgi calls a history-oriented human rights curriculum that focusses on universal human attributes, one in which the pupils identify with humanity as a historical reference point, rather than with a particular ethnic group (Georgi 2003: 315, 2009: 105). One has to be careful, however, and to look closely at how such a curriculum might actually function in order to guard against the occlusion of difference parading as universalism (cf. Yurdakul and Bodemann 2006).

Here is an illustrative example of some to the difficulties that can be encountered in just such an endeavor. A radio program on *Deutschlandfunk* describes a visit to Auschwitz by members of an organization called the Muslim Youth of Germany (MJD). One visitor, a high school student of Turkish-Arab background, begins:

> Since I grew up here in Germany. I never had this view of the Turks, as it were, or of the Arabs. I don't believe that such a view is different. Although I can say: It was not my ancestors, if one wants to. Nevertheless, I do now feel as a German, somehow a bit guilty, that I feel sorry for the people, and I think, how could the people be so cruel back then? And they are people just like me or like us, regardless of which ethnic group they belong to. (Kuhlmann 2011: 1)[4]

In this exchange, one can see how an attempt to approach this past from a human rights perspective can get entangled with tendencies, which rather than recognize difference as valid ways of looking to be integrated into a whole, try to erase them altogether. That is the assimilatory model at play: first, the young visitor denies having another (perhaps less valid) Arab or Turkish view, since he grew up in Germany. Then he goes on to negate that such a view would be different. Then he claims guilt. This young man seems to be performing quite a series of discursive strategies—all in an attempt to stake a claim to this story and form a sense of belonging as a rememberer. Such a human rights focus, while it may well embody a productive way out of the exclusionary dominant discourse of *Betroffenheit* on this topic, can be embedded in such an assimilationist context that it ends up functioning counter to pluralism in that it erases the differences rather than allowing them space and incorporating them into an integrative whole.

Meyer-Hamme (2009) recalls another thought-provoking and quite different position on this very issue. He cites a senior high school history student of Turkish background just about to undertake the *Abitur:*

> Yes, so certainly, you cannot, as a society, ignore that there are immigrants there with their own history … And demand that as an immigrant one practically, somehow strips of one's old history and steps into this costume of "German history." You can simply not demand this. And one has to, I think, what would be an important step forward, for example, for integration, that one becomes aware of the history of the immigrants too. (Meyer-Hamme 2009: 76)[5]

This young man's description and assertion is precisely to the point. First, the metaphor he uses of a "costume of German history" is particularly apt. His rejection of the assimilationist model is clear and adamant. It is, simply, too much to expect people "to step into this costume." He calls for a form of integration that I could relate to: a two-way process, in which the mainstream culture also has to move to appreciate the histories of the immigrants.

Such an integrative whole too needs to be flexible and receptive to those who want to join it and help form it, rather than perceiving difference necessarily as a threat, or an exotic appendage. What is and what is not compatible within such a whole, however, will have to be negotiated here on the ground with all the stakeholders. Certain views in the process would remain incompatible with such a consensus. Holocaust denial and blatant anti-Semitic attacks that demonize and dehumanize Jews (cf. Peck 2006: 109) come to mind. My point is that the discursive space has to be opened up to come up with the new forms in negotiation and consultation with the society at large, not only among the intellectual elites of German background—but it would, naturally, include them. Creating something new in this case entails taking risks, given the difficult heritage involved and the battleground that heritage can become.

A potentially fruitful model for constructing new inclusive remembrances might involve what Michael Rothberg has termed "multidirectional memory," where he calls for "nonappropriative hospitality to histories of the other" (Rothberg 2009: 25). Rothberg is taking a global view looking specifically at comparisons since the immediate postwar period between Holocaust memory and other memories of victimization. He argues that one might need to rethink comparisons as equated with sameness, but as tools to relating to history where "dissimilarity is taken for granted" (Rothberg 2009: 18). He argues, "understanding memory as multidirectional is ultimately preferable to models of competition, exclusivity, and exceptionality" (Rothberg 2009: 12).

I do find that this idea might be partially applied on this local-national stage. A most compelling argument in favor of such an approach—which ultimately might help in the process of redoing remembrance—is that "comparisons, analogies and other multi-directional invocations are an inevitable part of the struggle for justice" (Rothberg 2009: 29), justice here being defined as "parity of participation." Opening up the dialogue may indeed present risks, as already mentioned, but it also represents an opportunity to make remembrance act in the service of justice. It seems that some of what Rothberg is calling for is already underway. For example, cultural institutions, whose motives are generally seen to be beyond reproach, have already been making direct comparisons for some time now in the interests of justice. In 2005, the JMB hosted a "Darfur Week" during which drawings by children in refugee camps were exhibited, this an allusion to the drawings by the children from *Theresienstadt*. While the U.S. Holocaust Memorial Museum highlighted the victimizations in Darfur as: "It is never again all over again." Nevertheless, it must be kept in mind that such freedom to compare is not at all universal, as the firing of a German of Turkish origin in 2008 attests. The episode involved a comparison of racism in Europe today with anti-Semitism under the Nazis. Gilad Margalit recalls:

> While the German left adopts such a comparison … it evokes a sharp protest in the German political center and right, especially, when it comes from a German Turk who does not comply with German policy and is suspected of being a Turkish nationalist. In May 2008 Professor Taruk Sen, the director of the Center for Turkish Studies in Essen, published an article in an economics newspaper in Turkey, *Referans,* in support of a Jewish-Turkish entrepreneur, Ishak Alaton, who had complained in a letter to the same newspaper a month before about the growing ultra-nationalism in Turkey, which led to xenophobia and anti-Semitism. Sen compared the Turkish migrants in Europe (and not specifically Germany!) to the former Jews of the continent. This unfortunate declaration of Sen supplied the board of his institute with a pretext to dismiss him from his position … Even Sen's later distancing himself from his declaration did not change the decision. (2009: 223)

From my perspective, this is an illustration of power asymmetries that obtain a local particularity that any application of concepts of multidirectional memory, or any model of or potential movement toward a recognized diversity, will have to consider and negotiate in situ.

In terms of the JMB, it is also changing as I have outlined briefly above. The museum could well become a forum opening up discursive space. While a museum cannot be expected to solve much broader societal problems, the JMB might be in a position to interrogate them. This would require a strengthening of core competencies of empathy and self-confident openness throughout. Further, it would also call for an institutional awareness of, and resistance to, its own instrumentalization as a tool of coercive power.

Notes

1. Recall that I had originally wanted to include one more school in my study: a school from parts of Berlin that suffer from particularly high levels of neo-Nazism. After contacting all the *Gymnasium* and comprehensive schools leading to the *Abitur* in these areas, I did get one principal who expressed interest. He kept putting me off, however, mentioning he had not managed to find an

"appropriate class" to take part. I did follow up for a number of months, but then did eventually decide to give up. I had so much varied material already that I was not sure I needed, or could cope with, more. In hindsight, I am left wondering what he might have meant by a "fitting class." Might he too have wanted to lead me to the most appropriate performers he could find? This question, though, must remain speculation.

2. This is naturally not limited to the JMB, but is an issue in museum hiring practice more generally. Eithne Nightingale, for example, has made a similar appeal regarding British museums (Nightingale 2015: 610).

3. There are many differences that make wholesale comparisons, not to mention attempted applications, problematic; the main one, in my reading, is that the power relations are reversed. In a broad sense, immigration forms the "Canadian" nation. The structures were created over time in order to create new Canadians. Immigrants generally are not perceived as a threat to the nation. They make up the nation. This is not to say that inequalities among immigrants of different backgrounds, which favor immigrants of European descent, do not exist, but rather to stress that the structures that I had taken for granted were pragmatically constructed within a framework of deliberate immigration with a thought-through policy. The First Nations are most disadvantaged in comparison to the immigrants. They were indeed in my experience viewed, when at all visible, as "other" and even indeed exotic. This power asymmetry is reversed in Europe, where immigration was, and all too often still is, perceived as a threat to the nation. These structures developed over time and will take time and deliberate work to counter.

4. Weil ich hier in Deutschland aufgewachsen bin. Ich hatte nie diese Sicht der Türken, sag ich jetzt mal, oder der Araber. Ich glaub nicht, dass so eine Sicht anders ist. Wobei ich jetzt auch von mir sagen kann: Es waren nicht meine Vorfahren, wenn man es so will. Trotzdem fühle ich mich jetzt als Deutscher irgendwie ein bisschen schuldig, also dass mir die Leute leidtun, dass ich denke, wie konnten diese Leute so grausam sein zu der damaligen Zeit. Und es sind ja Menschen wie ich oder wie wir, egal, welcher Ethnie sie angehören.

5. Ja, also man kann als Gesellschaft auf jeden Fall nicht ignorieren, das da Einwanderer sind mit einer eigenen Geschichte ... Und man kann auch nicht verlangen, dass man praktisch als Einwanderer seine alte Geschichte irgendwie abstreift und in dieses Kostüm "Deutsche Geschichte" reinsteigt. Das kann man einfach nicht verlangen. Und man muss, ich finde, was ein wichtiger Schritt zum Beispiel für die Integration wäre, dass man die Geschichte der Einwanderer auch selber wahrnimmt.

Afterword

It has been many years now since I first voiced my desire to pass on a balanced understanding of what it can mean to contemplate this past to my children. Germany now faces new and ever-pressing challenges in terms of integration and inclusion of difference. Indeed, the influx of close to a million refugees, the increasing attacks on asylum seekers, a rise of overtly racist movements, and the growing success of an Islamophobic political party make the issues of belonging, as they arose in my research, all the more pressing. Who has access to political and cultural belonging? Can remembrance of the Holocaust be harnessed in the interests of social justice, rather than serving to confirm the already powerful in their political positions—as it did the children of German elites in my study? Perhaps, but for this to happen "Deutungsmacht"—that ever crucial power to interpret—will have to be shared more equitably.

I had, initially, been implicitly led by my own experience that differences could easily be combined into an integrated whole: as a child I myself could indeed identify with the "British," "Canadian," and the "Jewish" story. These had not been mutually exclusive. This journey in, through, and around the culture of memory here has shown me that this had been a naive assumption and that moreover, the models of belonging I grew up with were not to be simply and easily applied here. I do see that calls for an integration that I can relate to are being made here, especially by those who reject the either/or options—who reject the "costume of German history." These assimilative and exclusionary tendencies are conditioned rather than determined. My own path, beginning in Canada and now continuing here, has convinced me that there are possibilities to construct an approach to difference that is neither held in contempt, as the young "Neuköllners" were, nor exoticized as quaint, like the "Jews" portrayed in the museum with their strange eating customs, but that might be a part of a recognized whole. So, rather than simply pass on a balanced view of this past, I realize now that as my daughters mature I will need to work with them in order to actively build just such a view with the tools and networks that are at hand here in Berlin and beyond.

Berlin, 15 April 2017

Appendix

Questionnaire Use and Translation

I did, as an experiment, design a closed question version of the questionnaires putting in all the sorts of replies that I thought might come up. Comparing these expected replies to the range of variation that actually occurred reinforced my conviction that open questions had been appropriate, in that many more sorts of replies came up to several of the questions than I had been able to think of.

The issues such replies point to might have been obscured or invisible had I opted for closed questions. In constructing the questionnaires, I consulted some specific texts, my colleagues, and other experts in education who had experience working with teenagers on this topic. Using such open questions means, however, that it is not feasible to quantify the replies as such, as they can be so varied that they do not fit neatly into pre-given categories. This was a limitation that I was willing to accept. Indeed, the purpose of the questionnaire was to offer some contextual background, and to help in exploring the topic further, as opposed to crunching numbers. While some of the questions may have given the prospective visitors clues on what to look for, I found it crucial to have some notes on their previous positioning before the actual visit in order to better relate to how they conducted their visit. The foundation of the empirical research remains the in situ participant observations—what the pupils did much more than what they said or wrote.

Name or Pseudonym____________

Pre-visit Questionnaire

1.1 Age?

1.2 Gender?

1.3 Nationality (Ethnicity)?

1.4 Native language?

1.5 Religion?

1.6 Please check the statement that applies to you:

    I come from former West Berlin/West Germany _____

    I come from former East Berlin/East Germany _____

    I come from somewhere else (please give town and country)

    ____

1.7 Please check the statement that applies to you:

    My parents come from former West Berlin/West Germany _____

    My parents come from former East Berlin/East Germany _____

    My parents from somewhere else (please give town and country)

    ____

1.8 Is this your first visit to the Jewish Museum Berlin: yes/no? _____ If not, how many times have you been (including this visit)? _____

1.9 What expectations do you have for the visit?

1.10 What do you know already about Jewish history (what have you heard, read, watched)?

1.11 What feelings to you personally associate with Jewish history in Germany?

1.12 Please rank your interest in Jewish history in Germany on a scale from 1 to 5 (1 = no interest, 5 = a great deal of interest).

Name or Pseudonym from the first questionnaire_____________________

Post-visit Questionnaire

2.1 To which degree were your expectations met?

Please explain:

2.2 Did you have any unexpected experiences?

Please explain:

2.3 What were your predominant feelings in the underground sections? (The axes, the Holocaust Tower? In the Garden of Exile?)

2.4 What were your predominant feelings in the permanent exhibition section?

2.5 What does it mean to you, personally that this museum is in Berlin?

2.6 How did you find the visit generally?

2.7 Have your ideas about Jewish history in Germany changed as a result of your museum visit?

Please explain:

2.8 Have your feelings about Jewish history in Germany changed as a result of your museum visit?

Please explain:

2.9 Has your interest in Jewish history in Germany changed as a result of your museum visit?

Please explain:

2.10 What do you think you will most remember from your museum visit?

2.11 Would you be willing to be interviewed individually at a later date? If so, please leave contact details (telephone or e-mail). I will not give these details to any third party.

Bibliography

Assmann, Aleida. 2006. *Der lange Schatten der Vergangenheit. Erinnerungskultur und Geschichtspolitik.* Munich: C.H. Beck.

Bauer, Patrick. 2011. *Die Parallelklasse: Ahmed, ich und die anderen—Die Lüge von der Chancengleichheit.* Munich: Luchterand.

Bennett, Tony. 2006. "Exhibition, Difference, and the Logic of Culture." In *Museum Frictions: Public Cultures/Global Transformations,* edited by Ivan Karp, Corinne A. Kratz, Lynn Szwaja, and Thomas Ybarra-Frausto, 48–51. Durham, NC: Duke University Press.

Benz, Wolfgang. 2011. *Antisemitismus und "Islamkritik": Bilanz und Perspektive.* Berlin: Metropol.

Bishop Kendzia, Victoria. 2010. "Clichés Reinforced, Clichés Challenged. Visitors' Perceptions of the Jewish Museum Berlin." In *Cultural Representations of Jewishness at the Turn of the 21st Century,* edited by Madgalena Waligorska and Sophie Wagenhofer, 45–59. Florence: EUI Working Papers.

———. 2011. "Visitor Experience and Learning. The Case of the Jewish Museum Berlin." In *Forschungswerkstatt Geschichtsdidaktik 09,* edited by Jan Hodel and Beatrice Ziegler, 51–61. Bern: hep-Verlag AG.

———. 2012. "Site Affects: Room as Object: Reflections on some 'Confusion' in the Holocaust Tower in the Jewish Museum Berlin." In *Museum X. Zur Neuvermessung eines mehrdimensionalen Raumes,* edited by Fred von Bose, Kerstin Poehls, Franka Schneider, and Annett Schulze, 78–88. Berlin: Panama Verlag.

———. 2014. "'Jewish' Ethnic Options in Germany between Attribution and Choice. Auto-ethnographic Reflections at the Jewish Museum Berlin." *Anthropological Journal of European Cultures* 23 (2): 60–70.

Blumenthal, W. Michael. 2001. "'Wir sind ein deutsches Geschichtsmuseum' Interview by Judith Hart and Hans-Ulrich Dilmann." In *Spezial der Allgemeinen Jüdischen Wochenzeitung. Jüdisches Museum Berlin.* September/October 2001, 20–26. Berlin: Jüdisches Museum Berlin.

Bodemann, Y. Michal. 1996. *Gedächtnistheater. Die jüdische Gemeinschaft und ihre deutsche Erfindung.* Hamburg: Rotbuch.

———. 2002. *In den Wogen der Erinnerung. Jüdische Existenz in Deutschland.* Munich: DTV.

Bohnsack, Ralf. 2009. "Gruppendiskussion." In *Qualitative Forschung: Ein Handbuch,* edited by Uwe Flick, Ernst von Kardorff, and Ines Steinke, 369–83. Reinbeck: Rowohlt.

Borneman, John. 2002 "Deutschsein: Fiktion und das Reale." In *Inspecting Germany*, edited by Thomas Hauschild and B.J. Warneken, 173–94. Münster: Lit Verlag.

Bourdieu, Pierre. 1972. *Outline of a Theory of Practice.* Translated by Richard Nice. Cambridge: Cambridge University Press.

———. "Site Effects." In *The Weight of the World. Social Suffering in Contemporary Society*, edited by Pierre Bourdieu, Alain Accardo, Gabrielle Balazs, Stéphane Beaud, François Bonvin, Emmanuel Bourdieu, Philippe Bourgois, Sylvain Broccolichi, Patrick Champagne, Rosine Christin, Jean-Pierre Faguer, Sandrine Garcia, Remi Lenoir, Françoise Oeuvrard, Michel Pialoux, Louis Pinto, Denis Podalydès, Abdelmalek Sayad, Charles Soulié, Loïc J. D. Wacquant. Translated by Pricilla Pankhurst Ferguson, Susan Emanuel, Joe Johnson and Shoggy. T. Waryn. 123–29. Stanford, CA: Stanford University Press.

———. 2000. *Esquisse d'une théorie de la pratique précédé de trois études d'éthnologie Kabyle.* Paris: Editions de Seuil.

Brinkmann, Annette, Annegret Ehmann, Sybil Milton, Hanns-Fred Rathenow, and Regina Wyrwoll, eds. 2000. *Learning from History. The Nazi Era and the Holocaust in German Education.* Bonn: Arcult Media Verlag.

Broder, Henryk. 2001. "Es ist vergeblich". *Der Spiegel 39,* 24 September. 264–6.

Brodersen, Ingke, Rüdiger Dammann, and Signe Rossbach, eds. 2005. *Stories of an Exhibition. Two Millennia of German Jewish History.* 3rd ed. Berlin: Stiftung Jüdisches Museum.

Bruner, Edward. 2004. *Culture on Tour. Ethnographies of Travel.* Chicago: University of Chicago Press.

Clarke, Adele E. 2005. *Situational Analysis. Grounded Theory After the Postmodern Turn.* Thousand Oaks, CA: Sage.

Clifford, James. 1997. *Routes. Travel and Translation in the Late Twentieth Century.* Cambridge, MA: Harvard University Press.

Connerton, Paul. 1989. *How Societies Remember.* Cambridge: Cambridge University Press.

Converse, Jean M., and Stanley Presser. 1986. *Survey Questions. Handcrafting the Standardized Questionnaire.* Beverly Hills, CA: Sage.

Crapanzano, Vincent. 1992. *Hermes' Dilemma and Hamlet's Desire: On the Epistemology of Interpretation.* Cambridge, MA: Harvard University Press.

Davidson, Lee. 2015. "Visitor Studies: Toward a Culture of Reflective Practice and Critical Museology for the Visitor-Centered Museum." In *The International Handbooks of Museum Studies: Museum Practice,* edited by Conal McCarthy, 503–27. Oxford: Wiley-Blackwell.

Dekel, Irit. 2009. "Ways of Looking: Observation and Transformation at the Holocaust Memorial, Berlin." *Memory Studies* 2(1): 71–86.

———. 2011. "Mediated Space, Mediated Memory: New Archives at the Holocaust Memorial, Berlin." In *On Media Memory,* edited by Motti Neiger, Oren Meyers, and Eyal Zandberg, 265–77. New York: Palgrave Macmillan.

———. 2013. *Mediation at the Holocaust Memorial in Berlin.* New York: Palgrave Macmillan.

———. 2014. "Jews and Other Others at the Holocaust Memorial in Berlin." *Anthropological Journal of European Cultures* 23(2): 71–84.

———. 2016. "Subjects of Memory? Holocaust Memory in Two German Historical Museums." *Dapim: Studies on the Holocaust* 30: 1–19.

Denzin, Norman K. 1970. *Sociological Methods. A Sourcebook.* Chicago: Aldine.

Dewey, John. 1934. *Art as Experience.* New York: The Berkeley Publishing Group.

———. (1938) 1998. *Experience and Education.* Indianapolis, IN: Kappa Delta Pi.

Dick, Bob. 2005. "Grounded Theory a Thumbnail Sketch." Retrieved 28 July 2014 from http://www.aral.com.au/resources/grounded.html.

Diner, Dan. 1998. "Nation, Migration, and Memory. On Historical Concepts of Citizenship." In *Contellations. An International Journal of Critical and Democratic Theory.* 4(3): 293–306.

Ellis, Carolyn, Tony E. Adams, and Arthur P. Bochner. 2011. "Autoethnography: An Overview" [40 paragraphs]. *Forum Qualitative Sozialforschung / Forum: Qualitative Social Research* 12(1): art. 10. Retrieved 28 July 2013 from http://nbn-resolving.de/urn:nbn:de:0114-fqs1101108.

El-Tayeb, Fatima. 2016. *Undeutsch: Die Konstruktion des Anderen in der postmigrantischen Gesellschaft.* Bielefeld: Transcript.

Feldman, Jackie. 2008. *Above the Death Pits, Beneath the Flag. Youth Voyages to Poland and the Performance of Israeli National Identity.* New York: Berghahn Books.

Feldman, Jackie, and Anja Peleikis. 2014. "Performing the Hyphen: Engaging German-Jewishness at the Jewish Museum Berlin." *Anthropological Journal of European Cultures* 23(2): 43–59.

Flick, Uwe. 2009. "Triangulation in der qualitativen Forschung." In *Qualitative Forschung: Ein Handbuch,* edited by Uwe Flick, Ernst von Kardorff, and Ines Steinke, 309–18. Reinbeck: Rowohlt.

Foddy, William. 1993. *Constructing Questions for Interviews and Questionnaires. Theory and Practice in Social Research.* Cambridge: Cambridge University Press.

Fullbrook, Mary. 2002. *History of Germany: 1918–2000: The Divided Nation.* 2nd ed. Oxford: Blackwell.

Gable, Eric. 2010. "Ethnographie. Das Museum als Feld." In *Museumsanalyse. Methoden und Konturen eines neuen Forschungsfeldes,* edited by Joachim Baur, 95–119. Bielefeld: Transcript.

Georg, Karoline, Mirko Niehoff, and Aycan Demirel. 2009. "Multiperspektivische Bildungsarbeit. Das Beispiel der Kreuzberger Initiative gegen Antisemitismus (KIgA e.V.)." In *Crossover Geschichte. Historisches Bewusstsein Jugendlicher in der Einwanderungsgesellschaft,* edited by Viola B. Georgi and Rainer Ohliger, 221–36. Hamburg: Körber-Stiftung.

Georgi, Viola B. 2003. *Entliehene Erinnerung. Geschichtsbilder junger Migranten in Deutschland.* Hamburg: Hamburger Edition.

———. 2009. "'Ich kann mich für Dinge interessieren, für die sich jugendliche Deutsche auch interessieren.' Zur Bedeutung der NS-Geschichte und das

Holocaust für jugendliche aus Einwandererfamilien." In *Crossover Geschichte. Historisches Bewusstsein Jugendlicher in der Einwanderungsgesellschaft*, edited by Viola B. Georgi and Rainer Ohliger, 90–108. Hamburg: Körber-Stiftung.

Glaser, Barney, and Anselm Strauss. 1967. *The Discovery of Grounded Theory. Strategies for Qualitative Research*. New Brunswick: Aldine.

Goffman, Irving. 1963. *Behavior in Public Places. Notes on the Social Organization of Gatherings*. New York: Macmillan.

Gorbey, Ken. 2002. "Keynote Speech: 'Organising for Success in the 21st Century: A Challenge for Museum Leadership.'" Presented at the INTERCOM Conference Leadership in Museums, Dublin, Ireland, 16–19 October 2002. Retrieved 28 July 2013 from http://media.rcip-chin.gc.ca/ac/intercom/gorbey.html.

Gudehus, Christian. 2002. "Was bleibt, zählt. Kritische Überlegungen zum Jüdischen Museum Berlin." Retrieved 28 July 2013 from http://hsozkult .geschichte.hu-berlin.de/index.asp?type=rezausstellungen&id=8&view=pdf &pn=rezensionen.

———. 2006. *Dem Gedächtnis zuhören. Erzählungen über NS-Verbrechen und ihre Repräsentation in deutschen Gedenkstätten*. Essen: Klartext.

Habermas, Jürgen. 1995. "Was bedeutet 'Aufarbeitung der Vergangenheit' heute?" In *Die Normalität einer Berliner Republik: Kleine politischen Schriften VIII*, edited by Jürgen Habermas, 21–45. Frankfurt: Suhrkamp.

Halbwachs, Maurice. 1941. *La topographie légendaire des évangiles en terre sainte: Etude de mémoire collective*. Paris: Presses Universitaires de France.

———. 1952. *Les cadres sociaux de la mémoire*. Paris: Presses Universitaires de France.

Hall, Stuart. 1980. "Encoding/Decoding." In *Culture, Media, Language*, edited by Stuart Hall, 128–38. London: Hutchinson.

Herf, Jeffrey. 1997. *Divided Memory. The Nazi Past in the Two Germanys*. Cambridge, MA: Harvard University Press.

Herman, Edward S., and Noam Chomsky. (1988) 2002. *Manufacturing Consent. The Political Economy of the Mass-Media*. New York: Random House.

Herzfeld, Michael. 2005. *Cultural Intimacy. Social Poetics in the Nation-State*. Second Edition. New York: Routledge.

Hildenbrand, Bruno. 2009. "Anselm Strauss." In *Qualitative Forschung: Ein Handbuch*, edited by Uwe Flick, Ernst von Kardorff, and Ines Steinke, 32–42. Reinbeck: Rowohlt.

Hirsch, Marianne. 1992. *Family Frames. Photography, Narrative and Post Memory*. Cambridge, MA: Harvard University Press.

Hoffmann-Axthelm, Dieter. 1997. "Das Duodezfürstentum des Reiner Güntzer: Im Streit um das Jüdische Museum gibt es nur einen Ausweg: Die Auflösung des Kulturkombinats 'Stiftung Stadtmuseum.'" *Berliner Zeitung*. 16 July 1997, 25. Retrieved 28 July 2013 from http://www.berliner-zeitung .de/archiv/im-streit-um-das-juedische-museum-gibt-es-nur-einen-ausweg— die-aufloesung-des-kulturkombinats—stiftung-stadtmuseum—das-duodez fuerstentum-des-reiner-guentzer,10810590,9307204.htm.

Hooper-Greenhill, Eilean. 2006. "Studying Visitors." In *A Companion to Museum Studies,* edited by Sharon Macdonald, 363–76. Oxford: Blackwell.

Huhtamo, Erkki. 2015. "Museums, Interactivity, and the Tasks of 'Exhibition Anthropology'." In *The International Handbooks of Museum Studies: Museum Media,* edited by Michelle Henning, 259–78. Oxford: Wiley-Blackwell.

Kansteiner, Wulf. 2002. "Finding Meaning in Memory. A Methodological Critique of Collective Memory Studies." *History and Theory* 41: 179–97.

Kaschuba, Wolfgang. 2001. "Geschichtspolitik und Identitätspolitik. Nationale und ethnische Diskurse in Vergleich." In *Inszenierung des Nationalen. Geschichte, Kultur und die Politik der Identitäten am Ende des 20. Jahrhunderts,* edited by Beate Binder, Wolfgang Kaschuba, and Peter Niedermüller, 19–42. Cologne: Böhlau.

———. 2005. "Gedächtnislandschaften und Generationen." In *Der Nationalsozialismus im Spiegel des öffentlichen Gedächtnisses. Formen der Aufarbeitung und des Gedenkens,* edited by Petra Fank and Stefan Hördler, 183–96. Berlin: Metropol.

———. 2006. *Einführung in die Europäische Ethnologie.* 3rd ed. Munich: C.H. Beck.

Kessler, Judith. 2001. "Fromme Wünsche. Zwischen Resignation und Skepsis. Was jüdische Künstler vom neuen Museum erwarten." In *Spezial der Allgemeinen Jüdischen Wochenzeitung. Jüdisches Museum Berlin.* September/October 2001, 96–100. Berlin: Jüdisches Museum Berlin.

Kirchberg, Volker. 2004. "Repository of Memories or Catalyst of Illumination? Attitudes and Expectations towards the Jewish Museum Berlin among Generations and Classes." Presentation at the 98th Congress of the American Sociological Association (Cultural Sociology Section), Atlanta, Georgia, 17 August 2003. Retrieved 28 July 2013 from www.leuphana.de/fileadmin/user_upload/PERSONALPAGES/Fakultaet_1/Kichberg_Volker/files/Kirchberg_Jewish_Museum.pdf.

Kirshenblatt-Gimblett, Barbara. 1998. *Destination Culture. Tourism, Museums, and Heritage.* Berkeley: University of California Press.

———. 2000. "The Museum as Catalyst." Keynote address, Museums 2000: Confirmation or Challenge, organized by ICOM Sweden, the Swedish Museum Association and the Swedish Travelling Exhibition/Riksutställningar, Vadstena, 29 September 2000.

Klein, Julia M. 2001. "The Jewish Museum—'Not a Guilt Trip.'" *APF Reporter* 20 (1). Retrieved 28 July 2013 from http://aliciapatterson.org/stories/jewish-museum-berlin-%E2%80%93-not-guilt-trip.

Knigge, Volkhard. 2010. "Zur Ausstellung." Retrieved on 11 April 2017 from http://www.ausstellung-zwangsarbeit.org/stationen/juedisches-museum/eroeffnung-im-jmb/zur-ausstellung.

Knobloch, Charlotte. 2006. "Deutschland braucht einen neuen Patriotismus." *Zeit Online,* 29 September 2006. Retrieved 11 April 2017 from http://www.zeit.de/online/2006/40/dlf-schwarzrotgold-knobloch.

Koonz, Claudia. 1994. "Germany's Buchenwald: Whose Shrine? Whose Memory?" In *The Art of Memory: Holocaust Memorials in History,* edited by James E. Young, 111–19. New York: Prestel.

Korff, Gottfried. 2005. "Betörung durch Reflexion. Sechs um Exkurse ergänzte Bemerkungen zur epistemischen Anordnung von Dingen." In *Dingwelten. Das Museum als Erkenntnisort,* edited by Anke te Hessen and Petra Lutz, 89–107. Cologne: Böhlau.

Kouparanis, Panagiotis. 2008. "Guided Tours for Muslims in Berlin's Jewish Museum. Discovering a Different Belief." *Deutsche Welle / Qantara.de.* 3 September 2008. Translated by Aingeal Flanagan. Retrieved 27 July 2013 from http://en.qantara.de/wcsite.php?wc_c=8099.

Kugelmann, Cilly. 2001. "Keine Orte von Juden für Juden." In *Spezial der Allgemeinen Jüdischen Wochenzeitung. Jüdisches Museum Berlin.* September/October 2001, 12–18. Berlin: Jüdisches Museum Berlin.

Kuhlmann, Jan. 2011. "'Wie konnten diese Leute so grausam sein?' Junge Muslime lernen in Auschwitz über den Holocaust." *Aktuell-Archiv des früheren dradio.de-Auftritts.* Retrieved 27 March 2014 from http://www.dradio.de/aktuell/1600256/.

LeCouteur, Amanda and Martha Augoustinos. 2001. "The Language of Prejudice and Racism." In *Understanding Prejudice, Racism and Social Conflict,* edited by Martha Augoustinos and Katherine Reynolds, 215–230. London: Sage.

Lenhardt, Maya. 2009. "The Jewish Museum at the Juvenile Detention Center Berlin." *JMB Journal*: 5, 39–41.

Levy, Daniel, and Natan Sznaider. 2002. "Memory Unbound: The Holocaust and the Formation of Cosmopolitan Memory." *European Journal of Social Theory* 5(1): 87–106.

Libeskind, Daniel. 1991. *Between the Lines. Extension to the Berlin Museum with the Jewish Museum.* Amsterdam: Jewish Historical Museum.

Lindner, Rolf. 1981. "Die Angst des Forschers vor dem Feld." *Zeitschrift für Volkskunde* 77(1): 51–66.

MacCannell, Dean. 1976. *The Tourist. A New Theory of the Leisure Class.* New York: Schocken.

Macdonald, Sharon. 2002. *Behind the Scenes at the Science Museum.* Oxford: Berg.

———. 2006. Unpublished manuscript.

———. 2009. *Difficult Heritage. Negotiating the Nazi Past in Nuremberg and Beyond.* London: Routledge.

———. 2012. "Presencing Europe's Pasts." In *Blackwell Companion to the Anthropology of Europe,* edited by Ulrich Kockel, Mairead NicCraith, and Jonas Frykman, 233–52. Oxford: Blackwell.

———. 2013. *Memorylands: Heritage and Identity in Europe Today.* New York: Routledge.

Macdonald, Sharon, and Katja Fausser. 2000. "Towards 'European Historical Consciousness.'" In *Approaches to European Historical Consciousness. Reflections and Provocations,* edited by Sharon Macdonald, 9–30. Hamburg: Körber-Stiftung.

Mandel, Ruth. 2008. *Cosmopolitan Anxieties. Turkish Challenges to Citizenship and Belonging in Germany.* Durham, NC: Duke University Press.

Margalit, Gilad. 2009. "On Being Other in Post-Holocaust Germany—German-Turkish Intellectuals and the German Past." In *Tel Aviver Jahrbuch für deutsche Geschichte 37. Juden und Muslime in Deutschland Recht, Religion, Identität,* edited by José Brunner and Shai Lavi, 209–32. Tel Aviv: Wallstein.

Meyer-Hamme, Johannes. 2009. "Dieses Kostüm 'Deutsche Geschichte.' Historische Identitäten Jugendlicher in Deutschland." In *Crossover Geschichte. Historisches Bewusstsein Jugendlicher in der Einwanderungsgesellschaft,* edited by Viola B. Georgi and Rainer Ohliger, 75–89. Hamburg: Körber-Stiftung.

Mushaben, Joyce Marie. 2008. *The Changing Faces of Citizenship: Integration and Mobilization among Ethnic Minorities in Germany.* New York: Berghahn Books.

Nightingale, Eithne. 2015. "Afterword: The Continuing Struggle for Diversity and Equality." In *The International Handbooks of Museum Studies: Museum Practice,* edited by Conal McCarthy, 601–11. Oxford: Wiley-Blackwell.

Ostow, Robin. 1989. *Jews in Contemporary East Germany. The Children of Moses in the Land of Marx.* New York: St. Martin's Press.

———. 1996. *Juden aus der DDR und die deutsche Wiedervereinigung: Elf Gespräche.* Berlin: Wichern-Verlag.

———. 2001. "Reimagening Ravensbrück." *Journal of European Area Studies* 9 (1): 107–23.

———. 2007. "From Displaying 'Jewish' Art to (Re) Building German-Jewish History." In *Interrogating Race and Racism,* edited by Vijay Agnew, 298–320. Toronto: University of Toronto Press.

Partridge, Damani J. 2010. "Holocaust Mahnmal (Memorial): Monumental Memory Amidst Contemporary Race." *Comparative Studies in Society and History* 52 (4): 820–50.

———. 2015. "Monumental Memory, Moral Superiority, and Contemporary Disconnects: Racisms and Noncitizens in Europe, Then and Now." In *Spaces of Danger: Culture and Power in the Everyday,* edited by Heather Merrill and Lisa M. Hoffman, 101–32. Athens: University of Georgia Press.

Peck, Jeffrey M. 2006. *Being Jewish in the New Germany.* New Brunswick: Rutgers University Press.

Peleikis, Anja, and Jackie Feldman. 2013. "Der Shop als Spiegel des Museums: Ausstellungsobjekte, Souvenirs und Identitätspraktiken im Jüdischen Museum Berlin und im Yad Vashem, Jerusalem." In *Kultur all inclusive: Identität, Tradition und Kulturerbe im Zeitalter des Massentourismus,* edited by Burkhard Schnepel, Felix Girke, and Eva-Maria Knoll, 309–42. Bielefeld: Transcript.

Pieper, Katrin. 2006. *Die Musealisierung des Holocaust. Das Jüdische Museum Berlin und das U.S. Holocaust Memorial Museum in Washington D.C.* Cologne: Böhlau.

Purin, Bernhard. 2008. "Building a Jewish Museum in Germany in the Twenty-First Century." In *ReVisualizing National History. Museums and National Identities in Europe in the New Millennium,* edited by Robin Ostow, 139–56. Toronto: University of Toronto Press.

Quack, Sibylle. 2015. "The Holocaust Memorial in Berlin and Its Information Center: Concepts, Controversies, Reactions." In *The International Handbooks of Museum Studies: Museum Transformations,* edited by Annie E. Coombes and Ruth B. Phillips, 3–28. Oxford: Wiley-Blackwell.

Rogoff, Irit. 2002. "Hit and Run—Museums and Cultural Difference." *Art Journal* 61(3): 63–73.

Rothberg, Michael. 2009. *Multidirectional Memory. Remembering the Holocaust in the Age of Decolonization.* Stanford, CA: Stanford University Press.

Rothberg, Michael, and Yasemin Yildiz. 2011. "Memory Citizenship: Migrant Archives of Holocaust Remembrance in Contemporary Germany." *Parallax* 17(4): 32–48.

Sandell, Richard. 2007. *Museums, Prejudice and the Reframing Difference.* London: Routledge.

Schiffauer, Werner, Gerd Baumann, Riva Kastoryano and Steven Vertovec, eds. 2004. *Civil Enculturation, Nation-State, School and Ethnic Difference in The Netherlands, Britain, Germany and France.* New York: Berghahn Books.

Schuman, Howard, and Stanley Presser. 1981. *Questions and Answers in Attitude Surveys. Experiments on Question Form, Wording, and Context.* London: Academic Press.

Scott, Julie and Tom Selwyn, eds. 2010. *Thinking Through Tourism.* Oxford: Berg.

Simon, Roger I. 2005. *The Touch of the Past. Remembrance, Learning, and Ethics.* New York: Palgrave Macmillan.

Stass, Christian. 2010. "Was geht mich das noch an? Unsere Umfrage zeigt: Die NS-Zeit bewegt die Jugendlichen nach wie vor. Aber sie wollen nicht auf Befehl betroffen sein." *Zeit Online,* 4 November 2010, 1–8. Retrieved 28 July 2013 from http://www.zeit.de/2010/45/Erinnern-NS-Zeit-Jugendliche.

Strauss, Anselm, and Juliet Corbin, eds. 1990. *Basics of Qualitative Research: Grounded Theory Procedures and Techniques.* Newbury Park, CA: Sage.

———, eds. 1997. *Grounded Theory in Practice.* Thousand Oaks, CA: Sage.

Till, Karen E. 2005. *The New Berlin: Memory, Politics, Place.* Minneapolis: University of Minnesota Press.

Van Alphen, Ernst. 1997. *Caught by History: Holocaust Effects in Contemporary Art, Literature, and Theory.* Stanford, CA: Stanford University Press.

———. 2002. "Playing the Holocaust." In *Mirroring Evil. Nazi Imagery, Recent Art,* edited by Norman L. Kleeblatt, 65–83. New Brunswick, NJ: Rutgers University Press.

Waters, Mary C. 1990. *Ethnic Options. Choosing Identities in America.* Berkeley: University of California Press.

Welzer, Harald. 2010. "Erinnerungskultur und Zukunftsgedächtnis." Published on the website of the Bundeszentrale für politische Bildung. Retrieved 28 July 2013 from http://www.bpb.de/themen/ZL8DOO,0,0,Erinnerungskultur_und_Zukunftsged%E4chtnis.html

Welzer, Harald, Sabine Moller, and Karoline Tschuggnall. 2002. *"Opa war kein Nazi." Nationalsozialismus und Holocaust im Familiengedächtnis.* Frankfurt: Fischer.

Williams, Paul. 2007. *Memorial Museums. The Global Rush to Commemorate Atrocities*. New York: Bloomsbury.

Winter, Jay. 2008. "The Social Construction of Silence." Key Note Speech at the Conference: Cultural Memory. Forgetting to Remember. Remembering to Forget. Kent Institute for Advanced Studies in the Humanities, The University of Kent, 12 September 2008.

Winter, Jay, and Emmanuel Sivan, eds. 1999. *War and Remembrance in the Twentieth Century*. Cambridge: Cambridge University Press.

Wulff, Christian. 2010. "Andenken und Mahnung lebendig erhalten." Bundespräsidalamt: 1–3. Retrieved 11 April 2017 from http://www.bundespraesident .de/SharedDocs/Reden/DE/Christian-Wulff/Reden/2010/09/20100927_Re de_Anlage.pdf;jsessionid=A3F94499E73D208DF138247DBB35C814.1_ cid371?__blob=publicationFile&v=2.

Young, James E. 1988. *Writing and Rewriting the Holocaust. Narrative and the Consequences of Interpretation*. Bloomington: Indiana University Press.

———. *The Texture of Memory. Holocaust Memorials and Meaning*. New Haven, CT: Yale University Press.

———. 1994. "The Art of Memory. Holocaust Memorials in History." In *The Art of Memory: Holocaust Memorials in History*, edited by James E. Young, 19–38. Munich: Prestel.

———. 2000. *At Memory's Edge. After-Images of the Holocaust in Contemporary Art and Architecture*. New Haven, CT: Yale University Press.

Yurdakul, Gökçe, and Y. Michal Bodemann. 2006. "'We Don't Want to Be the Jews of Tomorrow' Jews and Turks in Germany after 9/11." *German Politics and Society* 79 (24) 2: 44–67.

www.ingramcontent.com/pod-product-compliance
Ingram Content Group UK Ltd.
Pitfield, Milton Keynes, MK11 3LW, UK
UKHW021911060726
69811PUK00004B/76